W9-CHH-731

COSTA RICA

GOOD STORIES REVEAL as much, or more, about a locale as any map or guidebook. Whereabouts Press is dedicated to publishing books that will enlighten a traveler to the soul of a place. By bringing a country's stories to the English-speaking reader, we hope to convey its culture through literature. Books from Whereabouts Press are essential companions for the curious traveler, and for the person who appreciates how fine writing enhances one's experiences in the world.

"Coming newly into Spanish, I lacked two essentials—a childhood in the language, which I could never acquire, and a sense of its literature, which I could."

—Alastair Reid, *Whereabouts: Notes on Being a Foreigner*

OTHER TRAVELER'S LITERARY COMPANIONS

Amsterdam	*Cuba*	*Japan*
Argentina	*France*	*Mexico*
Australia	*Greece*	*Prague*
Brazil	*India*	*South Africa*
Chile	*Ireland*	*Spain*
China	*Israel*	*Vienna*
Costa Rica	*Italy*	*Vietnam*

MOLLIE DONOVAN

COSTA RICA

A TRAVELER'S LITERARY COMPANION

(850) 776-8260
⌐ Please call if
found! ♡

EDITED BY

BARBARA RAS

FOREWORD BY

OSCAR ARIAS

WHEREABOUTS PRESS
BERKELEY, CALIFORNIA

Copyright © 2010 by Whereabouts Press

Preface © 2010 by Barbara Ras
Foreword © 2010 by Oscar Arias
(complete copyright information on page 236)

Map of Costa Rica by Bill Nelson

ALL RIGHTS RESERVED

Published by
Whereabouts Press
Berkeley, California
www.whereaboutspress.com

Distributed to the trade by PGW / Perseus Distribution

No part of this book may be reproduced in any form or by any electronic
or mechanical means, including information storage and retrieval sys-
tems, without permission in writing from the publisher, except by a re-
viewer, who may quote brief passages in a review.

Library of Congress Cataloging-in-Publication Data

Costa Rica : a traveler's literary companion /
edited by Barbara Ras; foreword by Oscar Arias
p.   cm.
PRINT ISBN 978-1-883513-00-9
EBOOK ISBN 978-0-9827852-0-1
1. Short stories, Costa Rican—Translations into English.
2. Costa Rican fiction—20th century—Translations into English.

I. Ras, Barbara.

To Helen and Henry, and in memory of Anna,
who traveled first

Contents

Map of Costa Rica   viii

Foreword   Oscar Arias   x

Preface   Barbara Ras   xiii

NORTHERN ZONE

Carmen Naranjo   *Believe It or Not*   1

José León Sánchez   *The Girl Who Came from the Moon*   10

Mario González Feo   *Bucho Vargas, Healer and Medicine Man*   24

SAN JOSÉ AND THE CENTRAL VALLEY

Yolanda Oreamuno   *The Lizard with the White Belly*   30

Rima de Vallbona   *The Chumico Tree*   34

Fabián Dobles   *The Targuá Tree*   37

Samuel Rovinski   *The Adventure*   43

Fernando Durán Ayanegui   *Monday*   55

Alfonso Chase   *Faust in Hatillo*   63

GUANACASTE

Rima de Vallbona   *Mystery Stone*   73

SOUTHERN PACIFIC COAST

Carlos Salazar Herrera   *The Bongo*   81

Alfonso Chase   *She Wore a Bikini*   85

SOUTHERN ZONE

Carlos Salazar Herrera   *The Carbonero*   101

ATLANTIC ZONE

Fabián Dobles   *The Diary*   110
Carlos Luis Fallas   *In the Shadow of the Banana Tree*   121
Quince Duncan   *The Oropéndolas*   134
Abel Pacheco   From *Deeper Than Skin*   136
Julieta Pinto   *The Blue Fish*   146

COSTA RICA

Yolanda Oreamuno   *The Spirit of My Land*   152
Carmen Lyra   *Pastor's Ten Little Old Men*   157
Joaquín Gutiérrez   *A Leaf of Air*   167
Max Jiménez   *The Palmitero*   191
Louis Ducoudray   *Here*   195
Uriel Quesada   *We Have Brought You the Sea*   202
Alfredo Aguilar   *Mint Flowers*   206
Carmen Naranjo   *When New Flowers Bloomed*   214

Glossary   221
About the Editors   226
Contributors   227
Translators   233
Permissions   236

V. Orosi

COSTA

V. Rincón de la Vieja

LLANURAS DE LOS GUATUSOS

CORDILLERA DE GUANACASTE

Golfo de
Papagayo

Liberia

Bagaces

V. Arenal

La Fortuna

Ciudad Quesada

Santa Cruz

Zarcero

Nicoya

Golfo de Nicoya

Chomes

San Ramón

Puntarenas

Orotina

PENINSULA DE NICOYA

Jacó

PACIFIC
OCEAN

0   10   20   30 miles

Foreword

Oscar Arias

If the attempt to describe physical reality in writing generally turns out to be less than fully successful, we would expect that a desire to apprehend reality through fiction would be similarly inadequate. Normally, the narrative is not history or geography or anthropology. Neither is it politics or economics. Why, therefore, should one seek in fiction a means for learning about a country or a national psyche? Why, when it comes to apprehending the reality of a region or a country, should we not simply resort to direct observation or, when that is not possible, to specialized texts that describe a place or a people from a scientific perspective—even, perhaps, reinforced with the luxury of statistics?

We are accustomed to seeing travelers and tourists exploring the woods, fields, rivers, and cities of our country, finding their way by means of maps, tourist guides, and hotel brochures and, in the unusual case, books and documents describing our very rich and abundant flora and fauna. This is only natural, since such sources help the visitor reach a deeper and more intense understanding of the landscape we Costa Ricans inhabit.

Some visitors also appear to be interested in our history, in the development of our political institutions and in the characteristics of our socioeconomic system. And they display a more than average curiosity when confronted with Costa Rica's institutional peculiarities, among them the pacifist and antimilitarist nature of our politics, our long democratic tradition, and our singular preoccupation with the education and health of our citizens. There are many publications that address these aspects of our reality, making it possible to develop a deeper appreciation of our nation.

One might think that the writings I have described would be sufficient for any visitor. Recently, however, Whereabouts Press set us thinking about the advantages of offering the traveler the opportunity to penetrate the Costa Rican soul and to plumb our most intimate reality through the many and varied paths of literature. Passing from concept to action, Whereabouts Press has produced this magnificent anthology of writing by Costa Rican authors under the title *Costa Rica: A Traveler's Literary Companion.*

The collection offers a broadly representative sampling of twentieth-century Costa Rican short fiction. The stories are of the highest literary quality, and they have been imaginatively organized according to the geographical allusions they contain. Given that Costa Rica is only slightly larger than nineteen thousand square miles, one might expect it would be difficult to identify diverse cultural literary specificities. It is well known, however, that our country occupies an isthmus and is in geological terms quite young—a combination which allows for a nearly unparalleled topographic, climatic, and biological diversity that has had important consequences for our people. It is not, therefore, surprising that Costa Rican writers reflect in their works the environmental and cultural differences that contribute to creating Costa Rica's collective identity. Their works take place in the plains of Guanacaste, in the high valleys of the central plateau, and in the flatlands of the north and the Caribbean coast. And as our biological diversity derives from bridging the southern and northern land masses of the American continent, Costa Rican culture today is the result of a convergence in which we note visible vestiges of Asiatic, African, American, and European cultures, blending with and characterized by adaptation to an exceptional natural world.

On a different plane, this anthology offers an accurate synthesis of the literary perceptions that accompanied Costa Rica's transition from a rural, rather isolationist, society at the beginning of the century to a highly urbanized society increasingly open to the cultural and commercial currents of the present decade of globalization. This transition, whether for good or ill, has brought with it a fundamental modification of the "Ticos'" relationship with their own surroundings and with the world at large.

May I add in passing that if one detects in these stories and tales various thematic, stylistic, and aesthetic correspondences with the literature of other Central American countries, only subtly do we begin to perceive the Costa Rican's mental adjustment to the new sociopolitical regional panorama in which dreams of autarchy and isolation—if, in fact, those dreams persist—have no place. Nevertheless, it is encouraging to me to observe that most of the living writers included here have, in different ways, supported the political actions that have led to peace in much of Central America and are now aimed at the political and cultural integration of the region.

I am sure that when travelers visit Costa Rica, they will receive a more authentic, more profound impression of our country and our society for having been in the company of the writers whose voices they encounter in *Costa Rica: A Traveler's Literary Companion*.

Translated by Margaret Sayers Peden

Preface

The first time I spoke with Carmen Naranjo, one of Costa Rica's leading writers, it was by telephone as I stood in the full Costa Rican sun at a public phone on a side street in Quepos, not far from Panadería Fiorela, the best bakery in town (the one that makes fabulous coconut concoctions *and* whole wheat bread). I was waiting for her to give me the address to her offices at EDUCA, the publishing house for seven Central American universities, and instead of a street number and name, she said, "La cuarta entrada de Los Yoses," or, roughly, "the fourth entrance in the neighborhood of the yos trees." Of course, I had no idea what she meant. (It's typical for San José addresses to be given in relative terms—500 meters from such and such a landmark is the norm—so my cab driver wasn't the least bit thrown by the destination I gave him.)

It was there, at "la cuarta entrada de Los Yoses," a phrase that for me has since taken on mantric qualities, that I met Carmen Naranjo, Julieta Pinto, Alfredo Aguilar, Floria Herrero, and others, writers who helped me find the entrances to Costa Rican literature, a body of work to match this astonishingly varied small land. From that meeting and from the names and books I took away with me resulted in *Costa Rica: A Traveler's Literary Companion*.

With the intent of making a representative sampling of contemporary Costa Rican fiction, I have tried to select stories that reflect the ethos of place, the country's biological, cultural, and geographical personality. I looked for pieces that unfold in particular locales, so that readers, whether traveling in fact or in mind, would find recognizable touchstones to guide them through Costa Rica's many regions, for here is a country that truly earns the name Rich Coast. Though around the size of West Virginia, Costa Rica has a chain of volcanoes and shorelines on both the Atlantic and Pacific. It is a nation with no army, where even common people in the outlying provinces are quick to say, "Our schools are our best defense." It is a country where stately palms grow in groves, row upon row, and where mountainsides are planted with coffee all the way to the dizzying top. It is a realm where the proliferation of fruits and flowers is the natural embodiment of deafening rain and blinding light.

Gathered here are stories that I hope suggest the spectacular variety of topography and wildlife, from San José, the capital, and the surrounding Central Valley to the savannas of Guanacaste and the lowlands of the Atlantic Zone along the Caribbean coast. Readers will find a number of words left in Spanish in the text and keyed to English in the glossary at the back, both for authenticity and to acquaint the traveler with common idiosyncratically Costa Rican expressions. Thus the ubiquitous "corner" store—the "tienda" of other Spanish-speaking countries—appears as it does in Costa Rica as the "pulpería." The national dish of fried rice and black beans, "gallo pinto," a favorite breakfast fare, appears untranslated, along with "pejibaye," the palm fruit that's a popular food nowhere else but Costa Rica. Various plants and animals are also given in Spanish in an attempt to make it easier for the traveler to identify unfamiliar species encountered on the road.

As in any collection containing realistic fiction, this one explores the great universals of love and work, rendered in fascinating particulars. Here is the obsessive nighttime monologue by the San José accountant in Samuel Rovinski's "The Adventure," who stays awake nights lusting after his wife's sister asleep alone in the bedroom down the hall. We meet the orphan in Carlos Salazar Herrera's "The Bongo," as she outwits the boatman on the Pacific Coast who imagines she has no choice but to marry him. Less fortunate is the eleven-year old in José León Sánchez's "The Girl Who Came from the Moon," who plots to escape her family's wrenching poverty and move in with a much older n'er-do-well. Here too is the romance between a young schoolteacher and a farm manager that brings new life to the mountain town in Carmen Naranjo's "When New Flowers Bloomed."

An astonishing variety of work is portrayed in these pieces, work that has a specific regional character, as demonstrated by the wandering gatherer of hearts of palm in "The Palmitero" and the poor campesino in "The Carbonero," who makes his living by burning oak for charcoal that he hauls to distant markets by donkey. Brought to life by Carlos Luis Fallas are the *linieros*, the railroad workers in the service of the United Fruit Company, whose labors are vividly evoked by "In the Shadow of the Banana Tree."

What is apparent time and again in these stories is the propensity for Costa Rican writers to champion the dispossessed. This keen social and political conscience is dramatized by Abel Pacheco in his vignettes about the blacks and whites in the Atlantic Zone around Limón and by Carmen Lyra in her poignant portrait of the relationship between the child of a rich land-owning family and one of its peons in "Pastor's Ten Little Old Men."

Of course natural wonders abound, and many stories reflect Costa Rica's vast panoply of flora and fauna. Carmen Naranjo's "Believe It or Not" features a hammock full of frogs, the "most naked creatures in the world." Yolanda Oreamuno enchants us with a fable of how the lizard, with the help of a humble Cartago woman, got its white belly. Quince Duncan weaves a tale around two youths and the oropéndolas, a bird related to our orioles, in a portrayal of the loss of innocence. In "The Blue Fish," a young boy on a childhood trip travels by a small low-flying plane from the capital to the Caribbean, where he is enthralled by a tauntingly beautiful fish he'll never forget.

In bringing out *Costa Rica: A Literary Traveler's Companion*, offered in the spirit of adventure and fulfillment, fulfillment of the promise of connection and knowledge that is the deep pleasure of the journey, I hope the reader will find any number of doors to the place called Costa Rica. Together with the colorful contours of the sites they illumine, may these stories reveal other entrances, crossing boundaries of maps, languages, and time, to open into love, work, endurance, instigations and insights, and those funny, healing moments common to us all.

I would like to mention a few titles that were a great help to me in editing this book: Carlos Gagini, *Diccionario de costa-rriqueñismos* (San José: Editorial Costa Rica, 1975); *Costa Rican Natural History*, ed. Daniel H. Janzen (Chicago: University of Chicago Press, 1983); F. Gary Stiles and Alexander Skutch, *A Guide to the Birds of Costa Rica*, with plates by Dana Gardner (Ithaca, N. Y.: Cornell University Press, 1989); *Narativa contemporanea de Costa Rica*, 2 vols., ed. Alfonso Chase (San José: Ministry of Culture, 1975), and *Antología de la lit-*

eratura costarricense, 2 vols., ed. Abelardo Bonilla (San José: Universidad Autónoma de Centro América, 1981).

I owe a personal debt to the many who helped to make this collection possible. My warmest thanks to the following colleagues and friends who enlightened or supported me along the way: Bill Turnbull, Ellen Watson, Stacy Shoemaker, Victor Perera, Amy Einsohn, Wilberth Alvarado, Alberta Rucker, César Hernández, Jean Pierre Larouchette, Luis García, Barbara Paschke, Paul Jenkins, Alfredo Aguilar, Floria Herrero, and Julieta Pinto. For valuable help with the glossary I would like to thank Marvalee Wake, Tony Avirgan, David Rains Wallace, Pedro León, Pía Porras, Elizabeth Braker, and Alex Alvarez Rojas. I am especially grateful to Emily Wheeler, for her steadfast presence; to Jeffry Glenn, whose love for Costa Rica is just one of the things we have shared in our longstanding friendship; to Carmen Naranjo, for her crucial support at the beginning and throughout the project; to Rima de Vallbona, for her willing and able responses to many pleas for help; to Alfonso Chase, for providing a constant measure for judgment and spirit; to Eduardo Cabrera, who resolved with great finesse a multitude of translation problems; to Ana Patricia Cartín and the staff of Editorial Costa Rica, for facilitating the complex task of permissions; to Will Kirkland, for his exquisite sense of how to proceed when all else failed me; to Alfred Rucker, the perfect editor's editor and much more; to Anna Rucker, for being there with love and joy; to Ellen Towell and David Peattie, my publishers at Whereabouts, for their generosity and vision; and to Oscar Arias, for his eloquent foreword and tireless work to further cross-cultural understanding and peace.

Barbara Ras

Believe It or Not

Carmen Naranjo

LA FORTUNA IS A TOWN in northern Costa Rica, near the border with Nicaragua. To get there, you have to curve right and left. Go up and down mountains. Touch clouds and shiver with cold. Sometimes, waterfalls thunder, other times, wide rivers flow with clear and resonant waters, occasionally, currents so deep that you can barely see the bottom from the tip-top of a narrow bridge sown with crosses in memory of accidents.

Coming down, you always arrive at a meeting of bridge and river, and going up, you always run into a cloud stuck to a mountain, which can spread out into mist for many miles of forced myopia.

More than a town, La Fortuna is a commercial center serving many farms, some large, some small. People on the farms begin work at sunup and worry about the livestock, planting bananas and yucca, snakes appearing (how dreadful!), poor don Albino (who died from the evil he saw), and the tales to be told at nightfall.

La Fortuna's most famous storyteller is don Fulminante; in fact, he's been nicknamed Fulminating Fib. He lives on a ranch exposed to the winds and sheets of rain that arrive every year without fail, beginning early in the morning, before breakfast, and frequently lasting all day.

He has two milk cows, three hounds he trained for hunting, a cornfield among the coconut palms, and a hammock, in which he takes his siesta and sleeps all night. Butterflies, lizards, cicadas, and even an occasional toad come and go happily on his ranch. But never snakes, because don Fulminante wears an amulet around his neck to protect himself from all venomous animals.

He's a vigorous, affectionate man, a good neighbor, always ready to do the right thing, a keen observer, and very clever with words. He knows how to tell a tale with the agility of a good bullfighter, seeking out the bull and then eluding it as if it weren't even there. What's more, he can do anything—fix pipes, build houses, repair machines, reduce the rate of drinking, relieve indigestion, and, in case of emergency, even bring babies into the world. There's nothing he can't do; he knows about electricity, mechanics, bricklaying; he even makes beautiful furniture, comfortable and long-lasting because he knows which woods to use, the ones immune to moths and other pests.

He became famous as a miracle worker when someone brought a ruined tractor to town and dumped it in the ditch. He started passing by it, casually, and quick as a wink it was good as new. Then he parked it near City Hall with a sign on it: "Whoever needs it can use it." That tractor has been used out of necessity for a lot of good work, because that was don Fulminante's mandate.

Every night, from Monday to Sunday, daily, without exception, the neighbors came by his ranch along with other folks just passing through who had heard of his reputation as a great storyteller. Don Fulminante greeted them all cheerfully, asking about their work, their health, what news there was from here and there. Like a good strategist, he let the audience fill up before he began his story; he knew that it would be retold all around. He had always known that stories break silence and nourish those who work, feel, and dream.

"You'll never believe this," he always began. "Well, I went to La Fortuna to buy some Alka-Seltzer, and I found that it was getting more and more expensive. So it occurred to me to rent that little ridge you see over there, so lovely, shapely, and fertile, and I planted it with great care, because in order to plant you have to love the earth, you must sing to it and enfold it. I set each tablet a foot and a half apart in the form of a circle, because the ridge lent itself to it and because the earth yields more when planted with beauty. You should have seen how the flowers and the birds expressed their thanks! I planted in April and waited for July to harvest those little Alka-Seltzers. But I didn't have the best luck. The weather betrayed me, as it betrays all *campesinos*. In May the sky began to cloud over and brought torrential rains; the hillside turned white and began to slide down in a white cloud that covered all the fields and highways. It was truly amazing. Let me tell you, it went all the way to Ciudad Quesada, more than forty miles from here. People still remember that fabulous event, because it was the first and only time in this area that it ever snowed."

After smiling with gleeful mischief, he began again. "You'll never believe this. One day, I decided to go fishing and I went to the banks of La Fortuna River. I had just arrived at the water's edge when I saw a big bunch of beautiful colored fish playing around, swimming back and forth, like children coming to life. I fell in love with one of them, the one with the biggest eyes. With great care and enthusiasm, I managed to put it into a jar. With even more effort and zeal, I set about teaching it to breathe out of water. Mouth to mouth I filled it with air, put it on the ground for a few minutes, and then put it back in the water. I repeated this process more than a hundred times, and finally the little rascal learned to breathe on its own. I brought it to the ranch and taught it to live with the hens, who at first treated it like a stranger but later became convinced that it was a poor plucked rooster. I also taught it to eat corn and *plátanos* and scratch for worms. Everything was going well and the little fish seemed very happy. It spent a year with me, and then the saddest thing happened. It was October. It started pouring rain early in the morning and didn't let up all day. The next day was worse. It was so bad that the dry gully you see over there turned into a river of raging water. The little fish fell in the swirling torrent and even though I jumped in after it, I couldn't save it. The poor thing had forgotten it was a fish and couldn't even remember how to swim."

The townspeople frequently said to each other that nights spent with don Fulminante were shorter and left them more cheerful.

First thing in the morning, the storyteller was up and about, taking care of thousands of chores. People wondered where he got time to make up his stories. Maybe with all the creative power he had, he could create time to work on his stories.

"You'll never believe this. One bright, cloudless day the sunlight was so brilliant and crystal clear that everything was transparent. I don't know if you've ever noticed, but there are days when the sun spends its time revealing everything. You can see the veins in the leaves, the sap that goes up and down branches, seeds inside fruit. Well, this light provided an irresistible temptation to go hunting and I invited my dogs to come along. I talk to them a lot—they're my friends and companions, the only family I have. They got excited and impatient, jumping up on two legs, dancing around and yapping. They love to run after game. I looked for my shotgun and went to load it. Bad luck! I had only one shell left, but I thought maybe by some miracle I would at least get a wild rabbit. Was I ever wrong! I set out on the road and at the first junction, I ran across a beautiful gaun. I took aim and bam! Shot it right in the heart. But the bird started running round the hillside; so, being neither sluggish nor lazy, I started running after it with my dogs. Tearing around the curves, the guan did in three rabbits I was tracking and finally reaching the river, it shoved a deer toward the water and the deer fell and broke its neck. I took the bird and the three rabbits home, so I could free my hands and go back and retrieve the deer. Feeling quite content, I set out on the road again, taking along that wheelbarrow you see over there. I didn't want to end up with a hernia from lifting that animal. Then I arrived at the river and was there ever a surprise in store for me! Really, you'll never believe it!"

Don Fulminante paused, wickedly watching the faces of his audience. Everyone was attentive and somewhat apprehensive of what the waters could have done to the deer.

"Well, I retrieved the deer very carefully. That animal was heavy! When I finally got it up on land, I noticed that four fish were stuck on each antler. For eight days straight I invited my neighbors for lunch and dinner. That's why they remember that lucky day very well, the day I bagged a guan, three rabbits, one deer, and eight fish with a single shot."

Nobody knew don Fulminante's age. He looked old yet

strong and full of life. He gave the impression of having been many places, something in his face and hands evoked an interminable road upon which he seemed to walk endlessly. His slanting eyes, surrounded by many wrinkles, gave glimpses of other lives, other times. They united distance and absence.

No one knew whether don Fulminante had any family or loved ones. He never mentioned anything about his past, except for his amazing adventures. He was respectful and affectionate with everyone. People felt like he was a relative, an immediate family member, a kind of soulmate. This added up to something, since without a doubt he was at the forefront of the town's cultural heritage and everyone looked up to him: the cowboys, the mule drivers, the shopkeepers, the tractor drivers, all those who at some time in the night or early morning invented stories of their own.

"You'll never believe this. One afternoon when I was coming down with malaria, the ordeal of the fever made me wrap myself up in a blanket and I lay down in my hammock. At some point, I don't know exactly when, a green frog with bulging eyes climbed in. It sat watching, hunched over with trepidation. I looked at it with enormous tenderness, and the frog relaxed to the point that it dared to wink. (Love, when you know how to express it, is the most binding element of all.) I slowly lowered my hand and it jumped at my touch. I began to caress it with devotion, and the frog responded by stretching out completely. What a lovely gesture, I thought. How can I respond? For the first time I realized, despite having seen so many frogs in my life, that here was the most naked creature in the world. It had nothing to cover itself with, no hair, no tail, not even thick skin. There it was, with nothing but the look of a frog, absolutely and chastely naked.

Then it occurred to me that I too should undress to make myself equal—nothing should stand between us. No sooner said than done: I stood there just the way I came into the world, though granted, older and larger in every way. The frog drew closer, as if it understood my gesture, and began to croak with a deep and pleasing sound. A chorus responded from different directions. The communication was perfect. At that moment—what a sight!—the hammock filled up with frogs and the first one to arrive began caressing my cheek. I couldn't move, because I didn't want to push anyone out; then another, almost by force, opened my mouth and leaped inside. I had to swallow it, because it was suffocating me, and when it moved deeper inside me, I felt my throat being shredded. Ever since then, a bit of frog has lived within me; lots of frogs follow me around with great confidence and no fear. Look how close they are—here, there, even on the roof. Ever since that time, I always take off all my clothes before I go to sleep, I like insects, and I hop around on the floor like they do, I also sing like they do. When I recounted this for the first time, someone who saw me with all these frogs following me around called me the Lord of the Frogs. That title doesn't bother me; when all is said and done, it's the only title I've ever earned in this so-called school of life."

Later, on the way home, one neighbor commented to another that the Lord of the Frogs seemed unaware that with immense love and admiration many called him Fulminating Fib. Because when a lie is an obvious exaggeration, it's as welcome as fresh fruit on a hot day. It spreads happiness, and that acknowledges what great tales don Fulminante told us. He would repeat old favorites without sparing any details or expressions. They said, for example, that don Fulminante had a way about him. Last night he told us that bees loved him so

much they made a honeycomb on his ceiling in the exact spot
for the honey to fall into his mouth when he was relaxing in
his hammock.

"You'll never believe this. Well, it so happened that one
of my molars began to hurt, one of these here in back. The
darned thing wouldn't leave me in peace. You know what
they say, if there's one sharp pain, there's always a worse one
sure to follow. The terrible thing is that it began to grow and I
couldn't even close my mouth. It hurt so much that I even had
to give up telling stories. To anyone who came by I held up
a sign that said: 'I can't talk, I'm temporarily mute.' I swear,
I even forgot what it was like to sleep, because as soon as I
closed my eyes, the cursed molar took delight in piercing my
jaw, and my ears filled up with a noise like a mining drill. My
face was so swollen that my nose disappeared; I had no profile
and looked like nothing more than a ball with ears. Faced
with this insufferable situation, I began to treat myself with
any medicinal plants that could bring me relief. I took bits
of *yerbabuena* with leaves of *reina de la noche*, which helped
me sleep. Feeling totally hopeless by now, I came to town
and looked for the dentist. He told me that he would have to
pull that miserable molar and to do that, the swelling in my
face had to go down. That was no easy task, but with hope,
prayers, and persuasive conversations with my own flesh, I
could finally see my nose, the same one that you see here
now. With my face recuperated and my molar shrunken, I
went back to the dentist, who assured me that it wouldn't hurt
much. He gave me a shot, which, let me tell you, was a prick
so sharp that my sphincter opened and I was terrified that I
would have the misfortune to let loose at that moment. How
embarrassing that would have been! Luckily, I put my right
hand here and was able to keep it all in. The dentist opened

my mouth, inserted the forceps, and began to exert some force. Nothing. The molar didn't budge. The damned thing was stubborn! The dentist then called his assistant and the two of them pulled. Nothing. The wretched thing was immobile. He called some other people and they started making a chain that filled up the clinic and stretched out for three blocks, all the way to the church. Everyone gave it their all. Nothing. Solid as a rock. Someone showed up with a team of oxen. To this day I still can't understand how they connected it to my molar. Neck and neck the two of them set out up the street until it felt like my molar was coming out. But it was a false sensation, an absolute illusion. The molar held tight until finally the connection broke. The dentist said to me, 'Look, don Fulminante, that molar is yours and doesn't want to leave you. You'd better stick with it. Even though I've never exerted such force before, and I've wasted the entire morning, you don't owe me a thing.' His recommendation seemed fine to me, and I stuck with the molar, which you can see is still there in one piece. Besides, ever since all that nonsense, it has never bothered me again or hurt one little bit."

"Don Fulminante, hello, how are you?"

"Very well, thanks. I'll expect you tonight, but you'll never believe . . . "

Translated by Barbara Paschke

The Girl Who Came from the Moon

José León Sánchez

Lord,
this is the story of my sister
who went away with a man
when she was eleven.
My sister was the mother of a girl
who left with a man
when she turned nine.
My niece has a girl . . .
Lord, Lord,
we need a school in our village,
a school, a school!

Christmas Letter, 1962

PEPITA IS CRYING.

Juanito is crying.

Rosario is next to me on the banks of the river playing with a ball of mud.

It's a ball of red mud from the river bank right here, because Mama says we don't have any money to buy real balls with.

Our *rancho* is up there. It's a *rancho* without any walls, made out of palm branches with pigs underneath it.

Everything, everything is mud.

It rains every day in the mountains, it rains every afternoon, it rains every morning, and at night it rains.

Chabelita is sitting on the palm-branch floor, covered with flies, yellow with pee, and her eyes are red from crying so much.

Pepita, Chabelita, Juanito, and Rosario are lucky because they can cry.

I never cry, and when I forget and I do, Mama hits me, and if she doesn't, Papa does.

Rosario isn't crying now.

Sometimes she doesn't cry, because she has a strange habit when she gets hurt of picking up some dirt in her hands and eating it and then she doesn't feel like crying.

Oh, I wish I could eat dirt like she does when I feel like crying!

Mama says that women don't ever cry.

Papa says that women shouldn't cry.

I'm a grown-up woman now, but I want to be like I was before. It was a long time ago that I was a little girl and I could cry about a lot of things like Chabelita is crying today, and sometimes she cries just because she likes to cry.

It used to be—but that was a long time ago—that if I was hungry, I would cry and they would give me something to eat. But that wouldn't do much good now, because sometimes there isn't anything to eat in our *rancho* and so, what good would crying do anyway?

A lot of times I feel a pressure in my eyes, like when the wind comes and the trees fall over and go from one side of the river to the other.

But who's ever seen a woman cry?

Not even when the pains hit Mama's big stomach three

times three, and she bites down on the wooden grater and lies down on the floor, does she cry.

Mama is a mountain woman, and mountain women don't cry.

I'm talking to you, river, who's always singing an endless combing-combing song on the roots of the plants that can see themselves in the mirror of your water, when it comes, when it goes, when it's gone . . .

I'm talking to the clouds that are way up, way up there, that drift in your current when the flowers fall from the *guarumo* trees and go floating by.

And I am talking about what is going through my mind now, like when a person is going crazy, going crazy . . .

Mama is very old now, and her hair is as white as the smoke from green wood, and her teeth have fallen out of her mouth, and her face is like where the lake runs out, all crossed with little wrinkles like those that cover the rivers, and only her eyes are still beautiful, so sweet and kind, where Papa can see himself and we can see ourselves, and from where, sometimes, it seems as though God is looking at us . . .

Sometimes they get all purple, and if I didn't know that women don't ever cry, I would say that some mornings I think that Mama drops her white hair, which is like the smoke from green wood, into the folds of her apron made from a burlap sack and cries without making any noise, like the wind when it plays alone over the tops of the trees.

But it's better not to think that, because it's a lie and a lie is as bad as the stinger of a bee . . .

Mama's stomach is always big.

One day I asked her why women sometimes have such big

stomachs, and then Papa took both my hands and put them over the hot coals of the cook-fire.

Mama's legs have little blue veins going all over them, and sometimes one of them pops out of the skin like it's a little marsh snake coiled up there. And when it does, it's hard for her to stand and she feels very bad.

I've never asked her why she has those little veins all puffed out like they were marsh snakes because Papa might be listening and take my hands and put them over the coals of the cook-fire again.

When Mama feels bad I make her better with pig lard, and then I tell her to lie down, and Rosario and I do all the work.

I said already there was lots to do on our *rancho*, and when Mama and Papa go to work in the mountains at four in the morning, I take care of the baby, wash the clothes, get firewood, make food, and scare away the pigs.

Mama works with the ax and the machete just like Papa does, and all the peons do. Some days Mama and Papa come back late at night with their clothes all wet and after they eat they lie down and go to sleep without saying anything to us at all, without giving us a hug or a smile or looking at us the way they sometimes do, and in a minute they are snoring so loud and I give the baby some sugar-water to suck on so her crying doesn't wake them up.

Sometimes I feel so tired, so tired. So very tired.

Mama never feels like this and even she says it's pretty strange, and when she hears me coughing she gets very sad and presses me against her heart, so sweetly that for sure it means something special.

The other women on this mountain never feel tired either.

For sure it's because one day I came from the moon . . .

My skin is white, as white as the face of the moon. The moon is the same color as corn when it's been boiled in ash.

Someone said once, "Micha seems like she doesn't have any blood."

Micha! That's what they call me now. A long time ago, when I was little, they called me Micaela.

Could it be that I came from the moon one day and that's why I don't have any blood?

Mama just looks at my white-yellow skin and says I must have something because the women from here don't usually have white skin, skin as white as mine. I've noticed that it really takes a lot for me to bleed, as if I didn't have any blood at all.

What happened in the pig hut when that rattlesnake bit me?

Ai-ai, my whole body gets bumpy, like the bottom of a washtub when I think about it!

It was a day like today when I spent the whole morning in the pig hut feeding the pigs we have for fattening—there are two and another in all—when I felt the rattlesnake-thing get me on the right foot.

Ai-ai, my skin turns bumpy, like the bottom of a washtub when I remember that!

See this scar I have here on my right foot? No, not that one. I got that one trimming off the firewood with an ax that wasn't very sharp. The other one, right here, is where Papa put his knife in, really deep, like he does when he cuts the fat pig's throat, and no blood came out. I screamed really long, really long, like a night without sleep, like a mountain reed, or like a monkey that's wounded and trapped in the branch of a tree.

And I think I screamed: "Owwww!" But I didn't cry. And then Papa killed the snake and carried me to the *rancho,* where Mama was waiting for me.

Papa put his mouth on the cut and drank from it, just like when we go on the little trails through the jungle and drink water from the reeds, or like the little pigs drink from their mother's belly.

A little while later some thick blood came out, and Papa spit it out of his mouth really fast.

Then Mama came and put a hot iron on the cut, red as the fire on the moon in the mornings sometimes when I get up to light the coals in the cook-fire, or like the deep red of the ribbon I saw once around the edge of a woman's dress in Grecia.

And then I don't remember anything else until I woke up in the Hospital at Alajuela.

I don't know how they got me there or which way they went. It had to be on their shoulders and then in a boat and then on a mule and then in a wagon until they got me to that bed in the Hospital at Alajuela where I spent the most wonderful days I have ever had in my life.

(Eusebio tells me I'm going to have other days as beautiful as those, but I don't believe there could ever be days as full of happiness as they were.)

Ah, I almost forgot to say it's really Eusebio I have to talk about, but in a little while!

When I was in the Hospital at Alajuela I didn't have to do anything except stay in bed all day. Here in the mountains, the women like me don't believe me when I tell them this. The women like me say it can't be true, that it's a lie, that it couldn't happen. But it really did!

I don't ever lie, because a lie is as bad as the stinger of a bee.

Everything was beautiful there and they gave me milk and candies and sweets and . . .

It was really, really beautiful!

They even gave me some honey as sweet as the honey the

bees hide in the heart of rotten trees, and they served it to me on a plate so pretty that I brought one of them back, and Papa hung it over the gate to our *rancho*, after making a little hole in it, so we would have a decoration.

When I woke up in the hospital (as I was saying and now I'll go on), I saw Papa looking at me with his eyes full of light like the moon when it makes the whole river into a wide, really wide, road, and it's easy to paddle all the way to the sea without needing a lamp on the bow of the boat.

When he looked at me, he didn't smile because Papa and Mama don't laugh very much and that makes them different from the people who live out there. But I saw that he was very happy in the way that people from the mountain have of being happy. But I got very sad when he told me we were coming back here.

No, no, never!

I've never had any bad feelings for that snake that almost killed me. Sometimes I even put my foot into some clumps of dead reed roots, right up to the knee, hoping that another rattlesnake will bite me and they'll run with me all the way to the Hospital at Alajuela.

Alajuela, oh how pretty, how pretty you are!

Once a poet came to our Witness Hall on a visit. (One of those people who say such nice words without a guitar.) He told how Alajuela was like the memory of a kiss that slid off the palm of a hand or like a dewdrop on the petals of a flower.

There, in Alajuela, the people aren't like over here. The men don't talk, or dress, or walk like Papa, they aren't like Papa. The women don't talk, don't dress like Mama, they aren't like Mama. And there's something very strange. They don't call women like me women: they call them girls. And these girls walk with other smaller girls in their arms, and the smaller ones seem really real and are dressed all in white and with pretty clothes that Rosario and I have never had, and their faces are painted like grown-up women, like they were made of week-old dough.

There in Alajuela the women like me (I said already that over there they are called girls) are taken by the hand everywhere, even to cross the street, or to go to the park where there are big trees like in the mountains and where girls with blue and white dresses with their arms filled with books walk around and around.

Yes, in Alajuela everything is very pretty, very pretty!

There the women like me don't know anything about anything. Not how to cook, or wash the clothes, or get the firewood, or cut bananas, or row a boat, and on top of all that they cry. They don't know how to walk in the mountains and they don't even know what a mountain is.

Ah, but what dresses they have, and what Mamas!

If the moon wanted to be nice to me, it would get another snake to bite me so I could go back to the Hospital at Alajuela for as long as I was there before.

I was there when I turned eight years old, and now I'm two years older, but I haven't grown very much and in those two years I haven't been able to forget all the pretty things I saw there.

But don't think they take you to the Hospital just for anything.

No, no way!

You have to have a tree fall on you, or a snake bite you, or a knife cut you.

Listen: If you ever know someone who gets bit by a snake or has the luck for an old tree to fall on top of them or gets cut by a machete, tell them to go to the Hospital at Alajuela.

They'll see how pretty, oh how pretty it is!

I came from the moon one day.

A while ago I asked Mama: "Mamacita, where did I come from?"

She looked at me with eyes that were purple that day, and wiped her hands that were black with dirt on her white hair, and she didn't understand my question.

I told her that everyone who lived on the mountain had come from somewhere else to live here. Eusebio, who I'm going to talk about pretty soon, came from the town of Tres Amigos on the river there in San Carlos; Anastasio, the one who brings the mail and comes up the river shouting "Riverboat's here, riverboat, riiiiverboat!" so that we go down and sell him some bananas, comes from the mountains near the volcano Poás, on up the river.

"You came from the moon, daughter," and Mama pointed at the moon.

The moon was in a sky that was almost night and almost day, like a blossom burst open on the pomegranate trees all around the Witness Hall where we Jehovah's Witnesses go once a month to pray for the poor people of the world, the poorest of the very poor, and we are living in these mountains here.

"One day I asked the moon for you, daughter." And she pointed at the moon again.

Now it didn't seem like a pomegranate blossom but a heart shaped like a ball, and I even looked at it again, affectionately, like I've looked so often at the face of my Mama, when I see it in those quiet moments in the middle of the river.

"We used to live all alone on the mountain, all alone . . . "

Mama began to tell the story and I began to dream.

Would it be as beautiful to live on the moon as to spend a month in a bed in the Hospital at Alajuela? Would everything there be as white and clean?

"I said to your Papa, 'We need a daughter.' And whenever the moon was shining on the water your Papa would stand on the river bank and look up and take off his sombrero and shout: 'We want a daughter, a daughter, a daughter for my wife and me!'

"And while he was shouting he would wave his sombrero all around the reflection of the moon in the water. He did this often when the moon was out, and one day the moon got dizzy from the sombrero and came down very quietly and left you on the bank of the river right here, and I picked you up. If your Papa hadn't gotten the moon dizzy with his sombrero, you would have stayed up there forever."

One day I asked her again: "What would you do, Mamacita, if I went back to the moon one day?"

Mama just looked at me like when she gives me one of those sweet caresses that must mean something special. She passed her hard hand very softly over my milk-white skin, and speaking very softly, softly she said: "If that happened, I would cry forever and ever . . . "

Papa and Mama love me a lot and that's why I don't understand why they hit me so much. Once Papa told Mama when I was trimming the firewood with the hatchet: "We are rich. Micha is our treasure."

Sometimes I think: If Mama and Papa are rich, why couldn't they buy the medicines that Señor Sarafín recommended to get rid of my cough that sometimes keeps me awake all night? If Mama and Papa are rich, why don't they buy something to stop my chest from hurting—like it did the afternoon when my hair got tangled up in a root in the bottom of the swimming hole down past the Villegas place where the river jumps like a snake and I almost drank all the water in the river?

No. I just don't understand.

Now I'm thinking about what Eusebio said to me.

Well, all right, the truth is that he's said it to me lots of times. I think he said it to me in that paper he sent with all those words and flowers and colored birds, too. I don't know what the paper said because I don't know how to read, but I gave it to Papa so he could tell me. Papa looked at it, then he looked at it again, and then he started talking to Mama without paying any attention to me: "This paper must be about love because there's a colored heart on it. I'll keep it so when I go by the Brother Evangelist's office he can read it to me."

The Brother Evangelist is the same one who reads the Bible out loud when we go to the Witness Hall and knows by heart the part that says: *"Blessed be those that weep, for . . . "*

What could that stuff about love be that Papa said the paper said? I have to ask Eusebio when I see him later.

One day Papa came back with a long face from the office where the Brother Evangelist works, and that very night I heard him talking to Mama: "Watch Micha very carefully, because she wants to leave us."

"Jesus, the things you come up with!" Mama answered.

"Watch her carefully, woman, watch her, because that tiger Eusebio is making his moves."

"That good-for-nothing who all the workers think is a

bum? And anyway, Micha's only a little girl, eleven years old and still flat in the chest."

"Just like you, woman, just like you, when you left with me . . ."

A hot cough came into my throat and I couldn't hear what they were saying anymore, though they stopped talking for a while when they knew I was awake.

I couldn't sleep that night and I spent hours coughing and coughing, thinking and thinking about what I had heard Papa say.

Well. It's true that Eusebio wants me to go away with him. He says that he's all alone on the *rancho* he built near the ravine with the *tepezcuintles*. I know he wants me to cook for him and wash his clothes and make him better when he gets sick, and he says he will never never hit me for anything like Papa does when he comes back from a visit with the rum bottle that Señor Jacinto has at the Blue Ravine.

So, if that's true, then: yes.

He also told me lots of nice things. That if the rice harvest comes out good he'll take me for a visit to Alajuela at the beginning of the year. He even knows the Plaza de Ganado, the Hospital, and once he made a visit to the Witness Hall there. He says he'll make me a real bed like the one in the Hospital at Alajuela and not out of palm fronds that the pigs knock over like the one I have now.

Some things about Eusebio I don't like, like the other day when he took my head in his hands and put his mouth on my mouth. I felt how those teeth of his, all black and dirty and ugly, hit my teeth, and I ran out to throw up behind a banana tree because it was really disgusting, and when I think about it now it makes me feel bad. But he told me that if I go with him we don't have to do that thing with his mouth against my mouth again because I told him that it makes me want to throw up and I don't like it, I really don't like it.

So, if that's true, then: yes.

Because I'm tired of working so hard. I'm tired of those coughing fits that take over my whole body even when I'm not near the smoke from the fire. I'm tired of not being able to cry or eat any dirt like my little sister does when I feel that pressure come between my eyes.

I'm tired of waiting for those days that come one after the other with all the humidity and so muck work.

At Eusebio's *rancho* I only have to work for him, and that's not very much, and I won't have to take care of anyone else but him.

So. I like that.

I know that Mama will cry, but I don't have any other choice but one of these two things: either go with Eusebio or go back to the moon.

Oh, how often I have asked the moon to take me back, and it hasn't even noticed me!

Now I'm talking about everything, like when someone goes crazy, goes crazy.

Rosario, the one who plays with balls of red mud, doesn't know.

Papa and Mama don't know.

The moon doesn't even pay any attention to me because it was dizzy when it left me here, and now it doesn't even remember me.

And that's why I'm going. I'm going with Eusebio because he promised never to hit me and to make a bed for me, all smooth and pretty like the ones in the Hospital at Alajuela.

He wants me to sleep with him in that bed too. And that's all right as long as at night when I'm sleeping he doesn't put his mouth against my mouth, because it makes me want to throw up.

That is what I am telling you moon, river, wind that blows . . .

Mama is going to cry because I am going away to Eusebio's *rancho*.

He is going to come in a few hours with a lamp in his hands to light our way.

He promised to take me by the hand tonight like the men do in Alajuela when they take the women like me across the road, the women who over there they call girls . . .

Translated by Will Kirkland

Bucho Vargas,
Healer and Medicine Man

Mario González Feo

I WAS A CHILD THEN and lived on a *finca* my father owned in San Vicente de Moravia.

My father put everything he earned doing business in San José into that ranch, or countryhouse, called María Luisa (which now in the depths of my memory, I remember as a garden of dreams, and in truth, that's what it was).

What's considered so new today, such as melons, "Washington" oranges, and Japanese peaches—all this and more—my father introduced to the fruit growers of the country. To do this scientifically, he brought in an expert from the Valenciana Orchards, don Matías Martí Rius, who from then on was considered part of the family.

Life has erased many things from my memory, but I will never forget don Matías's innocent blue eyes, the purity of his soul, that forbearance and resignation of his, so characteristically Spanish.

The wonderful thing about the *finca* was its irrigation system, installed by my father himself, having inherited from his Arabic ancestors the feel for handling water. He was helped in this by Jesús Venegas, his foreman, one of those loyal, responsible Costa Ricans—"gentlemen with both feet on the ground." CUTE SAYING

Completing the "community" was the inseparable Tista Sancho.

But on to the story.

Working in that house in the country was a girl—who was very pretty of course—called Challá. She had green eyes, dark hair with glints of copper, nice skin, and was mischievous and endearing.

It came to pass that this beautiful creature was struck with an attack of boils. First one would appear; then, when that one was on its way out, two more appeared to take its place; and in mathematical progression, those two were followed by four . . . and so on. The poor girl suffered unspeakably. They had tried every household remedy, even the darkest, stickiest spiderwebs that hung from the blackest beams of the kitchen ceiling.

But with the spiderwebs the household pharmacopoeia was exhausted.

Then she turned to Dr. Fonseca Gutiérrez, who besides being a doctor was a writer who signed himself with the pseudonym Jajaljit. But his prescriptions didn't do much to help her either. As a final resort, they brought Challá to the office of Dr. Elías Rojas, that pontiff of doctors, the perfect clinician, a gentleman without a flaw or a blemish. Dr. Rojas partially cured her with tonics and ointments, but the infection gradually returned, stronger than ever. Classical science, it's true, didn't have today's methods at its disposal, so doctors concentrated on doing what they could.

One afternoon, Papa was sitting on a bench on the porch, reading calmly in the shade of the fireworks vines. I was playing on the ground at his feet, watching, my mouth wide open (which was normal in children at the beginning of the century), the incredible speed of several red spiders, smaller than ants, that were "flying" across the rough brick floor.

Señora María (in those days, all the cooks were called Señora María) appeared and planted herself in front of Papa, looking very mysterious:

"Why don't you bring Challa to Bucho to be cured?"

"And who is Bucho?"

"Bucho Vargas is the be-all and end-all when it comes to curing every kind of illness. The person Bucho can't cure—and ask around if you don't believe me—is the person God wants to take back. Listen, he cured . . . "

(And she recited a long list of his miraculous cures.)

"All right, all right . . ." my father interrupted. "If you know him and he's the 'be-all and end-all,' as you say, tell him to come. 'May the miracle be done and may the devil do it.'"

The old woman, who was anxiously awaiting his permission, went running through a coffee grove in search of the miracle worker who lived nearby, along the highway to Carillo. Papa went on reading. I stayed right where I was and didn't even shut my mouth, in expectation of great things to come.

A little while later the old woman returned with Bucho.

He was a bit mestizo, short, square, chubby, oafish, as wise-cracking as they come, a sort of wild Sancho with an enormous goiter that he covered with a rolled-up handkerchief tied around his neck. He had obviously not heard of or practiced the old dictum "Medice cura te ipsum" (Doctor, cure thyself), for that phenomenal goiter just kept on growing. Besides that, he was a devout and prayerful man; one of those colorful and marvelous men of prayer from days gone by who would insert, between one mystery of the rosary and the next, a quatrain like this:

Medice cura te ipsum

The beads of my rosary   ARTILLERY ROUNDS
are artillery rounds,
and when my gun goes off
it sounds . . . Santa María! . . . etc., etc., etc.

He arrived carrying an immense umbrella, since it was raining. One of those solid, ample umbrellas as big as a circus tent, which people used to call bumbershoots, and which he would hold by the tip, letting the handle beat the ground. He had a pleasant laugh, ready and contagious, not at all the laugh of a simpleton. With natural grace and a good deal of ingenuity, he was the first to celebrate his every word. Which is to say, he would laugh at everything, and the truth be told, listening to him, one ended up finding everything amusing.

Bucho would cure his "patient" (though he said, more appropriately, his sick one, since if anything makes one not patient, it's to be in poor health), with procedures born of his many years as a health-giver. For someone on the edge of exhaustion because of a persistent case of the hiccups, he'd have the person stand for an hour (watch in hand), facing a whitewashed wall with his tongue flat against the white lime. (I now think the change in his pattern of breathing was surely what cured him.)

For erysipelas, an infection of the legs, he would rub the belly of an adult frog over the abscesses for a quick cure. Naturally, it had to be a different frog each time, since, as he explained it, after exposure to the disease the frog would carry it off and then "burst like a summer cicada."

For intestinal blockage, or the "colic miserere," he would prescribe slices of roasted eel to be eaten first in increasingly larger portions, which, as the "patient" improved, would be decreased. Since eels were abundant in our rivers, the prescription was easy and cheap. This was his internal therapy for the "miserere," and a small bagful of shaved ice on the right side of the stomach served as a local supplement.

He treated insomniacs with ease and cheer: the "patient" had to catch one hundred catfish in the Torres River and eat them, one a day. Or two. For earaches: two weeks listening to the murmur of the sea hidden in a shell for an hour a day. And so forth and so on . . .

Bucho made his assessment and gave his determination regarding Challa: she had a case of "perennial, effervescent boils of the humors."

When he looked at Challa, fear written all over her face, her green eyes wide, he said:

HUMOR

"You have eyes the color of parrot shit . . . ," followed by a burst of laughter. Everyone joined in.

Then he gave her a cursory examination, without paying undue attention yet without any prudishness either.

"All right now, Bucho," Papa said. "What do you think? Can you cure her? Yes or no?"

"Of course I can! And a good sight faster than you can imagine. This is nothing for me. Look, Challa: be grateful it's winter, because otherwise I wouldn't be lending a hand. When you see the rain running down the roads of the coffee plantation, drink a good pitcherful of it. Or even better, drink two. But it has to be water that comes out of the shadows and is collected right off the ground. The same thing every day . . . And then you'll have a story to tell me."

Papa was smiling under his mustache, as if to say: "I knew this Bucho wasn't a *curandero* or anything of the sort." My mouth was open wider than ever. Old María was in total agreement, without a doubt in her mind. And the rest of the household was in awe.

Challa, from the dark night of her suffering, glimpsed a miraculous light.

Bucho absolutely refused to accept anything for his visit and consultation. He only agreed to take a couple of big fat cigars after much insistence on Papa's part and after seeing how tempting they were. Off he went, with his laughter, his perpetual optimism, his good humor, his goiter, and his umbrella. *MARY POPPINS?*

No sooner did it start to rain than Challa would run to the coffee plantation and drink her two pitcherfuls of the water that flowed from the thickets.

That is how she was cured. In no time at all.

I'll say it once and say it again and clarify emphatically: "She was cured." Never again did she find even the trace of a boil. To the great joy of Señora María, the gratitude of Challa, and the stupefaction of the whole tribe, including Papa.

It was a miracle! . . . We had the distinct impression that the intelligent Bucho had made a pact with Mephistopheles.

Now, years later, remembering the incredible way the girl was healed, I think Bucho Vargas used the principle of terramycin and was nothing less than an unrecognized predecessor to Sir Alexander Fleming . . . And even Clorito Picado.

↳ *SCIENCE & BELEIF*

Translated by Mark Schafer

The Lizard with the White Belly

Yolanda Oreamuno

A story for men—children with big imaginations

For Kiko Quirós

THEY SAY THAT ONCE UPON A TIME there was a woman named doña Anacleta. They say doña Anacleta was the one who hid Morazán. In a cave. A very black cave, big no doubt, with huge boulders. In the heart of a mountain. Because mountains have a heart, I'm sure of that; what I'm not sure of is who doña Anacleta was and much less who was Morazán. I'm sorry to say that the cave is in Tres Ríos, not in Guanacaste. We're so used to looking for everything pretty, everything picturesque and quaint in Guanacaste; but I think that's a shame: the cave is definitely in Tres Ríos. Of course, there are no savannas in Tres Ríos that are covered with mud and water in winter and brimming over with sun in the summer; there are no savannas farther than the eye can see or mountains that spill over the wonder of the plain and stain it with bold stripes. None of that. But there are blue trees with purple trunks and there are mountains, yes, of course. And there are pretty corners of shade and little roads sketched in the pasture.

But that's what it's like now. In the "old days," I don't know. Because all this happened in the "old days" in Cartago. It takes place any time in history we like best; we can dress the ladies in crinoline and hoop skirts or put wimples on them. So, there was this lady down on her luck. That's how I understand it; the lady in the story was down on her luck, so she should first wear crinoline and hoop skirts and then, wimples. Well, it's not that important. The lady had daughters, too.

The daughters were in imminent danger. That goes without saying. There was no money in the house. Their moral balance . . . Well, their moral balance was at stake. You know what I mean. They were pretty and . . . starry-eyed, voluptuous. All of that must have made a pretty picture. Still—or maybe because of that—the lady suffered. Yes, she suffered a lot. She was afraid for her darlings, her good-natured daughters. Of course, men on horseback hung around wooing them and serenading them and the girls' petticoats must have been all aflutter. And they kept the place clean; since one had to cook, the other cleaned the house, and the other one . . . Well, I can't divide up the jobs since I don't know how many daughters there were. So, the lady went to the cave to beg the herm—I forgot to say that the cave had a hermit. And he was very good, and very skinny, and he talked very slowly, and in the afternoons he saw white angels. The cave had gray rocks and the hermit dreamed about God.

The lady went to him and begged him. The hermit prayed. He was always praying, he prayed with great faith. White angels spoke to him . . .

And then the hermit stretched out his hand. A sorcerer's hand, skinny and pale, with long nails like rivers on a brown land, with sinews straight like long seams, to give her the first thing he saw. At first his very blue, very knowing eyes transported him to heaven, then he lowered them, gliding over the walls, over all the earth, over the moss, over the dry leaves, and there—a lizard.

No doubt, he was to give the lizard to the lady. Of course, it didn't occur to the hermit how little the lizard was worth, because he stretched out his sorcerer's hand and the lizard became stiff, hard, cold, and heavy.

With her hands, the lady made a nest of shelter and credulity to receive it. She laced her fingers. Like this . . . One finger on top of the other, and her two palms hollowed out, shell-like and cracked. Her eyes brightened with admiration as she looked at the nest.

Then the hermit emptied out the strange jewel: the lizard's body was covered with emeralds from top to bottom, and its belly was no longer white.

And she left. Down the road sketched in the pasture, along the fence of trees like statues facing the little road.

And she went to the old miser with the hands of a saint to get the jewel appraised. But the lady didn't want that many doubloons or ounces, or the money of those "bygone days." She was satisfied with much less; much, much less. She was so ashamed of the amount that she refused to listen. So the old man plucked the emeralds from the lizard's belly. From the belly so it wasn't so noticeable and paid up.

The lady went home. Her good-natured, darling daughters, their petticoats all aflutter, married, of course, the gentlemen who wooed them on horseback and serenaded them at night. And the lady decided she didn't need anything else. That's how humble and happy she was. What more could she ask for? The next day she went up the little path to the mountain, her hands devoutly and lovingly made into a nest. A little nest of faith made with twigs of affection and warmed with tears of gratitude.

They say the hermit took the lizard with his sorcerer's hands and the lizard stopped being cold, inert, and heavy. And, they say, he set it on the ground and the lizard took off running.

They also say that since those "bygone days" all the lizards around the cave of gray stones and green moss, down the little paths of the mountain slope among the blue trees with purple trunks, where the lady climbed up and where the lady climbed down, those lizards have a green back and a white belly.

An old man tells this story. An old man with sorcerer's hands. And he says it's true.

Everything is simple and lulling and trembling. Like that . . . Well . . . soft and tranquil the way everything should be in those "bygone days."

Translated by Pamela Carmell

The Chumico Tree

Rima de Vallbona

PRESSED AGAINST THE RUN-DOWN schoolhouse, the chumico tree bears a miraculous fruit for the poor child who can't afford marbles.

When the poor child runs, the chumicos, black wealth of infinite roundness, fill his pockets with a muffled jingle, a chant of dreams, the anticipation of all the double shots that will fill the afternoon after hours of numbers, adjectives, northbound rivers, volcanoes: Poás, Barba, Irazú, Turrialba . . .

Ah, the delight of escape: now without hunger and poverty, past bare feet, ragged shirt, and patches, the boy opens the ritual by drawing the magic circle in the dust. Each hour turns into a whiff of time, a triumphant cry, a wild joy. Click . . . click . . . click . . . The chumicos boldly knock against each other in the magic circle of dust.

The recess bell rings and the children run to the chumico tree to see if it is finally time to pick its fruit.

"Here, Paco, one for me."

"No, you have too many. Throw me those three, Chalo."

"Pepe, don't be mean to me. Look, I don't have any."

"One. Just one for me," Anita begs timidly, trying to make herself heard over the shouts and uproar of the harvest.

"You want one?" Chalo looks scornfully at Anita's un-patched uniform, patent-leather shoes, and small, clean, white hands. Everyone looks at her like Chalo does, through the pride of their bare feet and their mended uniforms. From the top of the chumico tree, Chalo spits down at her, but she manages to dodge the spit.

"That's for you, shit-head! Have your rich daddy buy the chumicos with his money. If you come near here, you'll see what we'll give you."

On the way home, Anita wonders whether or not it's time for the first shoot of her penny tree to sprout. "Plant a few pennies and what a tree you'll have!" said Alma, the maid, Chalo's mother, who filled her imagination with stories of elves and ghosts. Anita planted her coins under the peach tree and waited impatiently with grand illusions. She waited, wishing that clocks and calendars would devour time until she would finally find herself on the highest limb of her penny tree, full of golden coins shining in the sun, ready for harvest. For you, Paco, for you, four pennies. And you, María, have seven so you won't push me or trip me. Here are nine pennies for you, Ofelia, but let me play ball. If you don't cuss at me anymore, Pepe, I'll give you ten. Chalo, Chalito, be good like your mother. Will you give me a chumico? Just one teeny-tiny chumico and I'll give you all the pennies you want.

Where Anita planted the coins, there is only a circle marked by stakes and the moistness of the ground, watered many times over with hopes that one day her hateful school-mates would say that she is equal to them, that they could all go together to splash in the Torres River and catch fish in the creeks, or slide barefoot on the black-green slimy gutters in town, or enter the magic circle to play marbles with the chumicos. Equal to them . . .

Meanwhile, from the distance created by her patent-leather shoes, Anita observes the children's game. Amid laughter and joy, click . . . click . . . click . . . , the black chumicos of infinite roundness bump each other within the circle until finally one knocks the other out of bounds. "A double shot? The chumicos chant promises of triumph.

From the bottom of her pockets, Anita's marbles—shining colors, infinitely round—do not chant promises of play, but they look very pretty. Clack . . . clack . . . clack . . . In the bottom of her pocket, Anita's marbles knock against each other.

The church clock strikes five, time for game's end, for goodbye, see-you-tomorrow; death of fantasy and laughter time.

The children, dirtier and more ragged, but all joy and noise, leave as they do every day. They rush to devour with endless hunger the thin soup made from bones reboiled for three days, the stew of *guineos* and the stale tortillas . . . if they are lucky enough to have even that left over from the day before.

Anita, always immaculate in her patent-leather shoes, leaves like they do, only silently and sadly. With little appetite, she sits down to eat the thick soup and tender meat smothered with rich gravy. And the penny tree that won't grow! "Will it grow, Alma, will it grow?"

"If you water it with faith and love, you'll see what a beautiful tree you'll have one of these days," said Alma.

In the midst of all this, the chumico tree keeps on growing and filling the poor children's pockets with dreams and hopes. The ritual of the game—of life—is performed again and again . . . but the penny tree still does not grow.

Translated by Mary Gomez Parham

The Targuá Tree
Fabián Dobles

FROM THE HEARTH, the eye of the fire stares out at the night and nods off to sleep to the sound of the coffeepot, which continues its rattling. Someone coughs—it's the loud cough of an old man behind whom a blurry hulk can be seen. Toward the corner an ember leaps into the air, stands still, then rises, lighting up the face of a woman who stands in the endless void of darkness surrounding her.

A neighborhood of crickets and shadows. The whisper of a brook at the foot of the hill. Trees fill their lungs with the wind. In front of the house a dog barks, a cow moos. Woven into the darkness and the stars, the mysterious murmur of night has set in. The chill of January.

In the doorway, beneath the edge of the black roof tiles, another old man appears unexpectedly. He makes a sign of greeting.

"*Buenas noches*," answer those within. Noiselessly, the old woman gets up as her husband asks:

"Who is it?"

The visitor hesitates in the glow of the candle just lighted by the woman, then crosses the room and, standing before the other man, says to him:

"It's me . . . Your brother Lolo." His voice quivers nervously.

A strange silence, solid and round, falls like a stone in their midst. His flaccid, bony face tenses up. His eyes want to speak, his ears moan to hear tongues suddenly run dry. Everything is transformed. Time has turned back, spinning wildly like a crazy top. Truth burns and goes out, like a bewildered half-burned log in their hearts. The three bodies tremble in the shadows like sails filled by a sudden breeze. Everything has become quiet and still as the two brothers stare, trying in vain to recognize each other beneath their deep wrinkles, everything in half-light—their eyes, the room, where like stanchions they stand facing each other. The one over here takes a step forward. We've said his skin is tense: his inner skin, the skin of memory, the one without a name, the untouchable one. The one over there, kneading his hat with his fingers, breaks suddenly into tears.

Time has stopped in its tracks, like the cat that settles on the hearth, its eyes lighting up like the last embers of the fire. The coffeepot is quiet, but the vision of time starts to boil, stirring up the past, searing with pain.

Everything had been forgotten. The years had worn down the rancor, turning it into a heap of hardened dreams, almost nonexistent. Now Lolo was here and suddenly that pile of dreams had awakened, writhing fiercely within.

The woman stood by silently, dissolving into the shadow.

Between their convulsive coughing and hesitant gestures, they spoke:

"I've come back, Chayo, because I didn't want what happened between us to keep eating away at me. We don't have a lot of time left, brother, and I didn't want to be buried still unhappy with you."

A glimmer—perhaps a smile?—appeared on his brother's wizened face. What difference did it make what they had said in the past? The important thing was that after all that time they embraced, there on the moist earthen floor, and they had to reach for their handkerchiefs because salty tears streamed down their cheeks, nesting in their yellowish mustaches.

I don't know why, but the cat came down from the hearth and rubbed up against Lolo's legs. The fire flared up, the coffeepot began to whistle—everything came alive again. Between the cigars and cups of coffee, nervous laughter and trembling, the three went to bed late that night.

"Forty years, brother," one said.

"And now you're alone. Just like me," mused the other.

"Yes, the children are grown. They're out on their own, running loose."

"We've been running loose, too, brother. Ever since we parted ways . . . "

One of the two, it doesn't matter which, was missing an arm.

The other had an enormous scar, like the largest of his wrinkles, that went from his nose to his ear.

In the wide valley below, the lights of the city sparkled, a myriad of tiny luminous frogs croaking in the pool of darkness. Here and there in the distance, patches of light could be seen, some weaker, others stronger. They all indicated the location of towns on the *meseta*, as if handfuls of stars had fallen from the constellations above. More than forty years ago there'd been fewer luminous frogs. San José wasn't as spread out then, and most people in the villages didn't have electricity. On a knoll of the hill behind which the house was situated, the *targuá* tree stretched upward, its old trunk smooth and its enormous leaves arranged in bright reds and oranges. From that rise you could look out on the valley as far and wide as the eye could see.

Chayo and Lolo had inherited the farm, pastureland, and mountains, along with some cattle and a few acres of coffee. Chayo, being married, was a man for work. Lolo, though not averse to using the machete and shovel, had a reputation for being lazy. He would pray and sing at weddings and burials, and at night he would often sit beneath the targuá tree, meditating all by himself. He liked watching the lights in the valley. On the boulder in the shade of the tree, he would wile away the hours, stung by the cold wind as he gazed below or played his guitar. Lord, how enraged Chayo would be if he found him there, wasting his time like an idiot.

"No, brother, I'm not wasting time. I'm honing it," Lolo would say, laughing, "the way you hone your knife on the sharpening stone."

"It's your rear end that's being honed on that boulder, brother," said the older one, his brow wrinkled in disgust.

But Lolo continued to believe that he was doing nothing more than carrying on the tradition begun by his dead father. Stretched out, his legs spread at an angle that took in the entire valley, he remembered his father that night long ago when for the first time the city sprang from the darkness with its yellow lights. Little by little, they appeared on all sides. Señor Concepción sat under the targuá tree with him and said:

"Those were the days, my boy, those were the days. Now we've got the railroad and light that travels along wires."

He lighted up a cigar and began to laugh wildly. After that, it was often that they sat like fools on that boulder, two peas in a pod. Once it occurred to the old man to say that all the lights were like frogs croaking in a huge pond. When the old man died, the frogs continued extending their domain over the valley, and Lolo sat and listened to them from the top of the rise.

It was just that Chayo, immersed in his work, his debts, and his harvests, didn't live for things like that. He said he was going to take his ax to the targuá tree to get a few cartloads of firewood.

"Father wouldn't have wanted us to cut it down," Lolo protested.

"Father is dead. I'm in charge now. Take a look at the damage the ants have caused that tree, the way it's drying out. We'd better make use of it while we can."

"Well, brother . . . ," he thought it over for a few seconds, as if hesitating to say what was on his mind. "But all this belongs to me, too, and . . . Leave me the tree. Leave me the tree and you can have the damn farm if you want it. I'll trade my share for the tree."

It was then that the hatred began to set in, because Chayo began to look at him silently, tensing up inside. Without answering, he withdrew. Lolo forgot about the incident, and set to fixing his guitar.

"The damn thing's gone sour," he grumbled.

But one day Chayo, stubborn as ever, came up with the idea that the targuá tree was sprouting the seeds of the strangler fig, posing a danger to the family land. His brother, distracted, didn't hear a word. God only knows where his mind must have been at that moment.

Months later, coming home late one night from a wake, Lolo looked up at the crest of the hill and saw that the targuá tree had become a pile of firewood. He sat on the boulder, downcast, his feet together, one drawn in against the other. He felt lonely. He spent the rest of the night brooding, brooding.

I don't know for sure if it was a sob, a cry, or a roar that came out of his throat when he met up with Chayo next to the house.

"Father didn't like taking the ax to the trees like that!"

One of them, I'm not sure which, is missing an arm. The other has a scar that time hasn't been able to erase.

Translated by John Incledon

The Adventure

Samuel Rovinski

THE HALL WAS FILLED with a tense, sticky darkness. The sheets rustled, squeezed tightly between his legs. His sweat was slow, gelatinous. Another night of his vigil, of a long, mortifying wait. The perfume was coming, he could smell it. He squeezed harder, he squeezed the sheets up into his groin, with an ache beginning to flood his loins. If it were her, ah, if it were her, for just a minute, one minute of grapevines, of wine and fire, and her for no one else but him. Her moist mouth coming to him, those full lips open so slightly, so red, waiting to be entered, the tongue approaching, seeking, pushing and twisting in, flexibly, skillfully. But no, it is her, fearful, teeth clenched, brow hardened, fear in her glance. The mouth opens, and—like that—wants to shout. A shout! Silence it. Stop it. No, it wasn't him, it was a dream. He feared the scandal, the shame wrapped in that shout, in that shout that would be heard across the flames of hell, in that hallucinatory intrusion into every silence, in that revelation of the most sacred secret of his desire. Quiet her, quiet her protest with a brush of his fingers alone, the simple sliding of his fingers over her skin, so smooth, so white, with the golden shafts in the field of downy hair still veiled from such caresses. And that scent, of young musk, so burning, rising from her sleeping flesh and clinging to the walls of his nostrils, making the cartilage tremble, wrapping it in shadow, in a hot cloud, to descend then, over the white hills, the broken lacework that shakes the recently opened earth, the warm dry clods. And then the sun, the red-and-yellow disk, an explosion of fire that would never again set behind the mountains, the same heat, the same rays that deform the already calcinated steel. A cloudless horizon, a burning yellow. Not even a small oasis or a mirage of shade to bring him thoughts of his life. And now, now he was so close, so close that his fingers pressed forward, pulled by the magnetism of her dark center, by the abundant wastelands he was breathing with indifference, almost in self-mockery, the sense of touch becoming paralyzed, crashing against an invisible obstacle. And the earth? The earth so newly yellow and dry, arid, cleared of grasses, cracking into millions of black furrows. And now? A drop that falls on the sheet, a quiet explosion of his molecules, a million atoms destroyed in silence. The white hills, the broken lace, wrinkled, the legs rubbing together, disturbing his guard. A cry of alarm and the field moves, shudders under the flow of drops that is now a gusher, the spasm that rises from the gorge, seeking the heights where the vertigo begins, the dizzying whirlpool that would carry him, carry him vertiginously along a sea of bursting foam. No, no more, it has to be stopped, it mustn't go on anymore, hold back, before it's too late!

It fell on his mouth like a thirst-stricken man falls on a ripe cluster of luxuriant juicy fruit. The skin of the peaches opened in a fan while the tongue made a circle, greedily, to recover the lost drops, searching inside, in a slow, studied curl. Now was not the time for lethargy. The limbs were growing longer, stretching out, filling with ants, thousands of them, stinging ants, industrious beneath their loads. A legion of stinging, maddened ants, making him lose his mind, lose himself in the hair beneath the arms, dizzy from the grotesque perfume, from the bittersweet perfume of the sleeping plants, silken, as those in a field bathed by a static moon, cold, absent, without a breath of wind, without the refreshing caress of the wind. Only a moan, an animal in heat, the irritated flesh, ready for a sudden attack.

Not a single particle of his skin moved.

The irritation made him turn toward the window. The curtains were slowly rising, moved by the pleasant night breeze, and the drawing of the square apples grimaced redly at him, an enormous smile vomited over his eyes opened wide by insomnia, by the torture of hours to come without sleep, with his teeth clenched together in the fruitless search for the desired prey, the loved one, the voluptuously yearned for, biting the impossible, struggling in the void.

He could almost see her, imagine her at the end of the hall, behind the half-open door, feel the palpitating signs of her hunger to be taken, make out the signs he had learned so well to decipher, her code of languid embraces and damp kisses. Oh! A paper his hands now wrinkled up in anger, a page of a lost language, a sexual palimpsest, a reiteration of gratification that was always learned anew. Ah! crumple up that paper in anger.

The wind lifts the curtain a few centimeters again, and the grimace stretches from side to side to laugh at his foolish face, at his shape like a cat ready to spring, at his glassy eyes, his thirsty, wet tongue.

Again he heard the toothed gears, one set of teeth against the other, with no beginning or end; only continuing, one mounted upon the other, seeking each other in their contours, one surface stuck to the other. Now, two of them becoming unstuck, but now two more beginning to join. One tooth meeting another, grinding, heavy, insistent, without any truce. One who receives without any pain, who accepts it as a necessary atavism of generative continuity, as an action that is not lost, a giving-in that is not wasted. The steel shines, polished and twinkling. The center of the gear pushes the entire mechanism harder and the sheets rustle, rustle, swirling like white hills now rising, now sinking without an oasis or a breath of wind or a drop of water to bathe the endless, split, dry furrows blackened by the hard metal in the road of sleep, of this sleep that won't come when his eyelids are heavy and weak and tell him that she is there waiting for him that her arms are languishing are opening like a flower to their gardener are stretching toward the infinite where the night hides the clamor of the endlessly quieted shouts in the wind in the wind alone that lifts the curtains a few centimeters toward that grimace of square apples that spit their scorn their mockery at him, ah!

At the end of the hall the shadows gather in a game of bodiless clowns. His eyes are opened again with insomnia.

If he hadn't interpreted those signs correctly, if that same morning he hadn't heard the solicitude of love in her words, there would be nothing now to indicate that she reciprocated. He couldn't have deceived himself. She loved him, he could be sure of that, but the path was difficult, and dangerous. Her breast had trembled near his, her breath, burning, had come with that message. He had discovered that life was filled with small signs to be decoded and that this woman, with a small gesture, from her silence, had agreed to give herself to him. And now she, like him (what wouldn't he give to be sure of this!), was suffering the torture of those wasted hours, of those days thrown into the wastebasket of routine. That morning, as on all previous mornings, the siren had howled the wakening of consciences, the return to the automatism of their duties. She had wakened the same person as always, the same figure, the same smile. But behind those masks, behind her greeting even, escaped from the superficiality of this picture, he had seen it, he had detected it: the sign! He had beheld it: her leaping heart. He found her resolved; an open confession was no longer necessary: he would have to be blind not to notice. But, what if he were wrong?

The picture over the chest of drawers, to the right; a little farther, books, magazines, bottles of creams, perfumes. Ah, and the chair: four legs, its red-and-gold striped cloth, a back worked in roses and arching branches, twining about, awful! Three hundred and twenty *colones* for that mess, another one of his wife's follies. His wife. And a son. The face beside him, that peaceful face, serene. She doesn't dream, is not tormented, surely; she doesn't have this fire of longing, of desire, like the fire that is devouring him second by second, night after night. If she knew, if she even guessed, there would be such a scandal, the stupid sobbing, the trying to hide from the accusing stares. "My God, what can I do, how can I repress this howl boiling up in me, pounding at my guts, hardening my sex, and clouding my understanding?" Remember that night, that night of their birthdays, the night they danced together and he discovered that he desired her. They were no longer simply a couple, she wasn't the woman he had courteously invited to dance, his wife's sister, at that table for three where she was growing supremely bored, looking around without seeing anything, yawning, dreaming, perhaps about a man. And he had invited her to dance and that enjoyment of her legs moving so firmly against his sex, the hard points of her nipples piercing into his chest; and he had to hypocritically disguise the desire aroused in him. A mistake, a terrible mistake. If this other face, lying next to his pillow, were to awake with the certitude of his love for her sister, it would be, it would be . . .

"Why had the accounts gotten so badly out of balance? Never had anything like this happened at Madrigal and Company, at least never in a way that was so ostensibly stupid, idiotic, infantile. Could he be losing his faculties? It's all this that keeps me from thinking anymore, won't let me concentrate on my work. I have to free myself, choose a love open to everyone's scrutiny, or secret rendezvous, or continence."

Simply leap out of bed, take a few steps and plunge into the adventure. His wife was snoring, snoring with satisfaction. Yes, the poor woman works hard, she does her utmost for the house and for them; he can't deny her virtue. And now, seeing her like that, her breast, almost naked, rising out of the blanket like a grapefruit wrapped in gauze, he knows she doesn't look all that bad, that she still has some of her charms. But she no longer attracts him as much. She is tired, always tired when they go to bed, and it takes a world of trouble to excite her. Her legs are heavy then, always rigid. The fire has disappeared, replaced by the silent, involuntary, friendly understanding they have forged, an armistice between companions, a coexistence between two worlds that barely understand one another in the silence. The attempt to recover that love, the passion of their early years, has disappeared. Neither of them makes the effort to reopen what has been locked behind a thousand doors, a thousand chains. "Damn her: I can't even despise her, hate her for those years pushed into the shadows, the same steps repeated mechanically over and over again. How can I tell her, how can I reveal this secret, this enormous and powerful passion that I feel for her sister? How can I tell her: I am no longer the one you thought you knew at your side all these years? It is over. We don't exist, we don't exist, how can I shout it? How can I make her understand? This bond that unites us is no longer sacred to me. Don't make the decision more difficult for me. I swear there's nothing sacred, nothing religious in it anymore. Now that this has burst upon me, there is only this: passion, desire, embrace her, enter her.

"She is an idiot, an ordinary and primitive being who is horrified by the thought of relationships outside of marriage. Her old ways of thinking, of restricting herself to the confines of morality have kept her from ever knowing happiness, the happiness that would have opened her up to surprise, to being carried away by the currents of desire, to loving freely and openly. But no, it is not she who thinks that way; when did I ever know how she thinks? It is me, it is the way I think, my own sensible moral code. I am afraid of a scandal, I am afraid to leave my own routine. There are other women, there are other adventures, and yet my eyes are fixated on this thicken-ing desire, on the torment of a night of love never realized because she doesn't know I love her. Where, where did I ever see in her glance that message, that promise of a night of intertwined bodies, of damp mouths and trembling to the ends of our fingertips?

"One leap, a few steps, in silence, without fear, and everything will begin to change, hurled into the whirlpool, dragged by the storm. Now we are here, together, so close together, no one can hear us; she moans, she embraces me, she says things into my ear I have never heard from the lips of my wife; she enjoys it, she writhes, her eyes are almost closed, close to climaxing, our limbs so intertwined they are deformed, and the leaves are falling, falling into a deep hole, and the trunk is growing bigger by the moment, seeking the sun, its enormous blazing roundness; burning; and the birds are flying everywhere in noisy flocks; near the sea, black reefs toss the waves, making them burst onto a huge continent of foam, white and boiling. A few steps and we are suddenly into the adventure. Ah, her skin, her cool skin, so eager . . . "

He threw the damp sheets to one side, turned slowly toward the edge of the bed and got up, trying not to make any noise. The distance between him and the door was getting bigger by the minute, an awful void. In the middle of that silence, in the center of that darkness, he could feel thousands of eyes on him, following, one by one, even his most imperceptible movements; they peered into his very guts, twisting in a spasm of fear. If she woke up, if she opened her eyes, that shape of a fearful cat, that cat about to leap, would surprise her for only a moment; and then the question, the stupid question, and he wouldn't know what to answer. He cast off his fear and took a step. He moved toward the door, supporting himself on the tips of his toes. It wasn't hard to walk in the dark through this room he knew by heart, its every corner, its every object recorded in his vigilant memory that for days and months had forged the same strategy, had gone over and over this exact plan.

It had to be resolved tonight. The idea of putting off the encounter was a nightmare, a horrible nightmare of a long new wait.

At the end of the hallway, behind that other door, expectant, anxious, she was waiting for him.

His wife was snoring. She mumbled something incomprehensible as she rolled over onto her other side. The sheets rustled.

His fingers closed around the doorjamb. He was standing in the middle of the doorway, his pajamas stuck to his sweating body. The chill of the mosaic floor began to rise through his legs and bring on the pain. Rheumatism stabbed at his knees and pressed in at his intestines. His hands stuck with cold sweat along the wood walls that ran the length of the hallway. He skillfully avoided all of the pictures hanging on the wall and reached the door of the other bedroom, half-open. It was always half-open, every night; she was terrified of being closed in, like in a tomb, as she had said so often. He pressed lightly on the panel and looked in. His heart beat harder and his breathing got faster and more out of control. His eyes peered through the shadows and there, behind a thousand shapeless forms, phantoms of the night, he could see her. She was sleeping. She was sleeping peacefully. She wasn't waiting for him! She was sleeping. She had not noticed his desire. She hadn't even felt his presence.

The loud exhaust of an early morning automobile mingled with the curse that sprang from him, just barely suppressed. She had been making fun of him! She had been playing with his feelings, with his desire. He could take it no longer. He would have her right there: silence her protests with his kisses, with embraces, with loving promises, and she would say yes, would abandon herself to his arms. He took another step forward, but he could go no farther.

The noise from the automobile trailing off through the San José night, a night of crickets and cicadas, provided a cover for his retreat, his bitter and discouraged defeat. The adventure had been greater than his strength could bear, too much for the obscure personality of a man of routine, of a man shaped for one life, for the same life, the endless life where every day was the same as the one that went before it. Perhaps someone else, in his place, with fewer scruples, would have thrown himself into it, would have taken the path that seemed to be the easier one; would have let himself go in the rivers of pleasure, without worrying about the consequences, without weighing his obligations. Ah, but not him, he is not so irresponsible. What would happen to his unsullied name, his career with the most important accounting firm in the country?

He went back to bed and collapsed, drained by his failure, exhausted by the tension. His eyes, wide open, filled with tears. Happiness, a happiness armed so patiently all through the years of his marriage, was beside him again. His wife, his wife was sleeping, innocently, peacefully. He tightened his fists with contained rage, with the shame of the unsatisfied male.

A dog howled in the street, recalling the moments spent with its mate. It was panting, panting with its tongue hanging out and drooling . . .

Sobs in the silence, offended dignity absorbed in the darkness, without witnesses, without explanation. But a moment later the colt races off in unchecked flight, sweating, neighing at the moon; muted orb, white, silent. His hand moves between the silk and the skin, squeezes the breast, caresses the sleeping nipple with his fingertips. Seeks out the well-known corners, the way to pleasure trod like an automaton for twenty years. The relaxed body grows restless and turns over. He presses against her back, waits awhile but gets no response. He presses harder. It is the same flesh, they are sisters; there is no difference. But that isn't true! They are different. By taking his wife he violates the sister, he sees her face in this sleeping one, underneath the features that are not the same; enjoys the one in the other, bites the flesh his fingers used to caress, discovers new life in the old places, young musk, drunkenly, fields plowed in the beginning of time, for the first time, light twinkling, dizziness from the pounding waves, earth that swells when touched by water, seed that grows abundantly, splendidly.

The curtains have stopped moving. Silence. The earth is asleep. One more truce. Daylight approaches and then night will come again, and another try, perhaps the last one or the resolution.

His eyelids grow heavy, they close. He sleeps.

Buses, cars, students, vendors, sweat, sorrows, joy, litter, have come again to the streets. The Vargas's house reflects the detail of its walls toward the outside. A lizard, nervous and frightened, pokes its tiny head, the head of a humbled monster, in through the red-black stones of the garden.

The glass of the milk bottles clangs against the tile of the entryway announcing the beginning of a hot new day.

Coming into the hallway, he catches sight of the two women chatting over breakfast. He carefully avoids being seen by them and goes into the bathroom. He fears that one of them may have discovered his nightly excursions, destroying the spell of his secret adventure.

Here, in the light of day, faced with the materialization of his dreams, pushed up against reality, his spirit weakens, is forced to a halt. His sister-in-law is not the one his imagination had drawn in the shadows. The one seated at the table, having breakfast, pleasantly conversing with his wife, doesn't give off any magnetic vibrations; is not the spellbinder who has enchanted him, who has pushed him to the edge of an adventure; has not, now, the magnetic center that so fatally draws him. There, seated, she represents the ties of family, the sacred totem, the iron prohibition of society, the sin.

When he greets her, which he will do, fatally, as he does every day, all his anxieties will reappear. Her gestures, her smile, her good morning, her normal conversation will be signals, signs for an encounter that will be delayed, deferred night after night. Her face, her hands, her hair, those cheerful eyes, that scent of her skin, that youthful figure, that enchanting virgin, will hound him relentlessly through the labyrinth of numbers at Madrigal and Company, through the narrow streets of San José. An obsessive image, repeated in the sky, in the mountains, in the stones, in the cups of coffee. A torturing image. Why doesn't she take the first step, why doesn't she free him of his cowardice? If she only knew what he was thinking, would consider being his lover. Ah, if he could only penetrate her thoughts!

After leaving the bathroom, finishing breakfast, and saying good-bye to his wife and sister-in-law, Miguel Vargas wasn't able to hear a conversation that would have satisfied his longing.

"For me, my dear sister, what I like are men who are decisive, happy, who don't ask permission for everything, who don't hide their intentions, who know to take you when they sense you are ready for love. Beneath the courteous man, the polite man, the one who flatters you with good manners, there is a wolf with his teeth broken off by the fear of punishment. I prefer the one who declares, once and for all, his intentions, who declares his love for you without any pretense, without any hypocritical veils."

Miguel is going to his office now, while his sister-in-law, a demonstrator of the excellent qualities of the beauty products Joie d'amour starts walking, looking ahead, luminously, toward a life of promises and dreams.

Then night will come, the curtains will lift lightly and a grimace of square apples will skewer its ecstatic smile through the man's face; and the adventure, the new adventure, will have begun again.

Translated by Will Kirkland

Monday

Fernando Durán Ayanegui

THE GARAGE WAS A DIRTY SHED that rose beneath a rusty old zinc roof on a dusty plot of land cruelly discolored by the constant drip of motor oil. Only a small surface was covered by a slab of coarse pavement mapped with fine, irregular cracks. Inside you could see a German tractor impossible to fix for lack of parts, a Ford of indistinguishable color, and a bus whose wooden chassis was destroyed; and everywhere, in disorder and abandon, there were abundant metallic parts, rusty to the eye.

From his spot Adán could see the street and hear everything that happened outside the garage. The whining buzz of the oil factory nearby was interrupted for an instant by the quick blast of a siren, which was echoed in another factory, in a theater, and which emerged moments later from the cathedral as three clean, resonant peals of a bell.

He saw his wife walk by. Despite his awkward position—half his body stuck beneath that dilapidated Ford—he managed to get a full view of her so he could make a fairly accurate guess at what was going to happen. Not long afterward he saw Mario Solano walking behind her; neither of the two appeared concerned about having passed in front of the garage. He was also sure that his co-workers had been sizing up the situation on their own, and that certainty upset him. He dragged himself across a large oil stain under the car and delicately mopped the sweat from his brow with the back of his hand, leaving his forehead covered with a black stain of rust, dust, and oil. The filth on his face gave him a ferocious appearance that had nothing to do with his heavy spirit. He wiped his hands on the thighs of his overalls, took a wrench from one of the tool racks, and walked to the door.

As he walked out he noticed that Héctor was watching him, curious. Héctor was a tall, gawky fellow who worked in the garage as a welder.

"So you've been spying on me, you son of a bitch," he said between his teeth and returned to place the tool on the rack.

"So you were spying on me," he repeated and slid back under the car.

There, lying on the nauseating concoction of dust and oil, he felt miserably tempted to imagine what was going on in his house. And it wasn't difficult, since similar incidents had happened many times before, and not only with Mario Solano. Anyway, Mario seemed to be her favorite, and she didn't think twice before going to find him at the butcher shop where he worked. So everything happened as if it were all very natural, as if they had just passed by together, one behind the other, only because they wanted to have fun and take advantage of the heat of the afternoon.

And it was really hot. It was the August heat of Alajuela, tinged in that part of the city by the endless snorting of the oil factory. At night the asthmatic wheeze of the boiler could be heard clearly, and in the afternoon, under the intense sun that made roofs sizzle, the mechanical sound of the factory seemed to represent the spasmodic breathing of an animal in agony. A yearning for rain swelled up in the form of human sloth under the barely clouded sky.

"I'm gonna go smoke a *Ticos*," Héctor said. They had agreed not to smoke in the garage. To smoke, you had to go out to the street.

"There goes that wretch saying he's going to smoke," Adán thought, "and now he'll wait outside until he sees them go in and he's gonna laugh at me like an idiot."

He no longer remembered how it all started. When he found out for the first time that his wife went out in the afternoons in search of men, he decided that the problem was too complicated to try to solve all at once. He made it his business to find a solution that didn't demand a lot of effort, and he found it convenient to wait until one day when he would catch them together at home. But almost consciously he had avoided leaving the garage any time she might be accompanied. The heat stripped him of his boldness, and he kept thinking there would come a better time to put an end to the problem.

Nevertheless, he now wondered why they insisted on acting so brazenly. It seemed like they wanted to provoke him. He wondered why they didn't try going somewhere other than his own house, or at least choose another path to avoid complications.

Héctor was smoking outside the garage. The other mechanic was tinkering with the bus engine, and it was easy to see that nobody felt like working on such a hot afternoon. In the Parque Central, without a doubt, under the giant mango trees, policemen, the druggist, shoeshine boys, a few students, and numerous beggars fanning the flies away with their open, bony hands would be resting like animals in a zoo. Meanwhile the cantinas would be deserted, because the drunks preferred to go doze on the lawn in the Parque Juan Santamaría; along the sidewalks of the marketplace you could see the drowsy faces of lottery sellers and the many people who made a living there by mysterious means. In all of the city there wasn't anyone who felt like working, and those who were, gnashed their teeth and muttered stupid opinions about preposterous issues while they endured the interminable buzzing of the flies and the frequent gusts, loaded with pestilence, that came from the slaughterhouse and a few clandestine pork butcheries. Suspended between the overheated blue sky and the earth's cover of sweaty human moss, buzzards slithered in tight flocks.

Adán didn't understand why his wife yearned for the company of another man, especially on an afternoon when you could hardly breathe. From under the car he felt the presence of the city squashed by the heat and imagined with absolute precision what would be going on at that moment in his house. Aurelia would have stripped off most of her clothes and would be fixing a drink for Mario Solano. The man would be anxiously awaiting the moment to go with her to the bedroom, and there Adán would find her if he finally decided to go and finish it once and for all.

Héctor tossed his cigarette butt and, pausing in the doorway, cast a malicious glance toward his co-worker, who was trying to tighten a nut. Adán saw it and felt obliged to curse him again.

"So they've already gone in," he said to himself. "You've got a good view from the door of the garage, so you know they've gone in together and they're cuckolding me again. That idiotic look on your face tells me so, and I know you're laughing to yourself and you think I'm a coward."

But he wasn't any coward. Strictly speaking, he wasn't. His wife's behavior caused him great pain, and he felt he had courage enough to go, one of these afternoons, and smash Mario Solano's skull, or anybody else's. It was just that he didn't want things to get complicated; besides, he knew that sooner or later he'd find an opportunity to root out the evil weed that had been planted in his house. It was lucky that he held himself back. He was simply waiting, and one of these days it wouldn't be hot enough to keep him from setting his wife straight. Anyway, at that moment, Aurelia would be enjoying the afternoon, and since it wasn't the first time that something like this had happened, it didn't matter enough to make him desperate. The opportunity would come, and he was sure he could take advantage of it.

"Aren't you gonna go have coffee?" Héctor asked.

Adán pretended to ignore the thrust of the question and didn't respond.

"It's after three," the welder insisted. "You're not gonna have coffee?"

He didn't want to answer—he knew exactly what Héctor was trying to suggest. He didn't want to say that he never went home for coffee in the middle of the afternoon for fear of walking in on his wife having a good time. But Héctor's question had made him feel humiliated, and for a few seconds he couldn't think clearly.

"Yeah, I'm on my way," he said suddenly, without being sure of what he'd do.

He dragged himself over the oil stain again, stood up—without bothering to wipe his hands on the thighs of his overalls—walked decidedly toward the tool rack, and grabbed a wrench.

Héctor saw him leave and didn't intend to stop him. For

a better view, he went back over to the door and waited patiently.

Adán walked with animal slowness along the dusty street of trodden stones mixed with sand and crushed brick. He brandished the heavy tool in one hand, rubbing the other against the bib of his overalls. He crossed the train tracks along the side street and was still ten meters from his house when he heard the buzz of familiar voices nearby. They were walking, balancing on the rails and jumping over the ties, a dozen men who all looked like workers. The leader of the march had a mesh sack thrown over his shoulder that held three deformed soccer balls.

"Hey! We thought you were gonna practice," shouted the one with the balls.

Adán remembered that the next Sunday was the neighborhood championship soccer game, and they had planned to hold a few workouts over the course of the week. Before he could answer, he heard another voice in the group:

"Remember, we've gotta play those Plaza Iglesias boys tough."

"They're a bunch of pussies!" someone shouted.

"I'll be there in a little while," Adán assured them, continuing on his way.

"But don't forget, cause we're gonna need you."

"I'll be right there," he repeated. "I'll be there as soon as I take care of some unfinished business."

"It better be quick," the man with the balls insisted as he walked away.

He grasped the copperplated doorknob. He entered without a sound and closed the door behind him with painstaking slowness. He tiptoed into the kitchen where he noticed the inevitable disorder of dirty cups and plates along with an incipient rotten smell coming from the trash can. He pondered what he would do once face-to-face with Mario Solano, but he didn't decide immediately. He was surprised to discover that he wasn't feeling particularly indignant, and this pleased him because now he'd be able to act reasonably, without doing anything rash. He approached the bedroom and was startled when the floorboards creaked lightly under his weight. He paused, held his breath, and slid forward with his back against the wall. The bedroom door was half open. He positioned himself so he could look inside with a simple tilt of his head. In the shadows of the bedroom the two bodies blended together on the bed, and in their joining he couldn't help but note an intriguing plasticity. He decided the wrench wasn't appropriate and returned to the kitchen to leave it on the table.

He quickly reviewed the various items chaotically arranged along the wall: a coffee grinder, the empty first aid kit, a cast-iron pan, several bottles, a pile of newspapers, an electric iron, and the kerosene tin. He found a cardboard box under the ironing board where beneath some bug powder his wife kept the old rags she used to clean the floor. He took several pieces of cloth and dampened them one by one with a fine stream of kerosene. As he began to breathe in the familiar hydrocarbon fumes, he worried that the smell would awaken the pair in the bedroom. So he hurriedly distributed the dripping rags in such a way that, once lit, no one would have a chance of escaping.

The air had grown pretty foul and became unbearable. He opened the front door, lit a match, knelt down on the floor-boards, and tossed the glowing flame on the nearest rags.

He left the house and headed toward the soccer field. As

he passed the garage he knew his co-workers were watching him, but he kept on walking, unperturbed. Before turning at the end of the street he looked back once more at the door of his house: no signs yet of the fire.

As soon as he reached the field, they put him on one of the teams. He took his position without having a well-defined plan. He carefully watched the game unfold and made sure he knew all the players. Twice he had the chance to get to the ball and take a shot, but he held back—better not to act too recklessly at first. He saw one of his teammates race down the field gracefully controlling the ball, never letting it get more than a few inches away from him. He felt an intense emotion when the ball rose a few seconds later, describing a delicate arc that came to an end in the arms of the goalkeeper.

Now he decided he was ready to act, and he confidently waited for the ball. He saw it coming; he took a few strides forward, came to a quick stop, and trapped it between his foot and the ground. Calmly, he advanced a few meters, stopped, and looked up to study the other players' positions. Without hesitation, he moved in a straight line toward the opposing net. He made a move for a shot on goal, but his view was momentarily blocked by one of the opposing players. So he passed the ball over to his team's left wing and, once open himself, moved in front of the net. When his teammate kicked the ball in a long trajectory, all he had to do was lift his foot to correct its path and score his first goal.

He strode proudly toward the center of the field while the few spectators suddenly drifted away, drawn by screams in the distance. Then he knew that everything had ignited as planned and, smiling openly, he felt relieved of a heavy worry.

Translated by Kirk Anderson

Faust in Hatillo

Alfonso Chase

HE WAS FIRST SEEN near Sagrada Familia, the church. Close to where the Lisbeth movie theater used to be. Later he went down toward the river, walking through the roughest, wildest parts of town, as if looking for an address or perhaps a vacant house. At least that was what doña Agripina said when the neighbors asked her about the strange visitor. She said he was fair-skinned. Like a German. Or perhaps a missionary, one of those who have taken to wandering through here with their pack of lies. But not in my house. No! We're Catholic, Apostolic, and Roman, no matter how many Bibles and leaflets and even used clothing they're giving away . . .

Wasn't he dark-skinned, though, like an olive? asked Zoraida, who used to hit the street when things got rough and Ramiro went on one of his two-week binges. The man was dark, and he had a mole near his lip. And he was wearing sandals, with the nicest feet, she insisted. I don't think he was dark, still less, fair. He was a bit pallid. Oh, yes, he wore sandals, and his toenails were quite long, but what I noticed most were his hands: so well cared for, as if he had never worked. As if he was used to having his nails done, as the little girl Betty said.

No one knew what this man was like before he knocked on Faust's door, then in Hatillo, and the story poured out all over the neighborhood, together with the rich fragrance of chorizo, *gallo pinto*, and the milk that inevitably spatters the whole kitchen . . . I don't remember what he looked like. But he was neither fair nor dark, much less pallid. His color was something like one of those figurines made by local artisans, but what caught my attention most was his hair: as if the wind could never muss it up, as Faust said when he was asked about the man a few months later.

After, he had left that neighborhood and started up his shoe repair shop again in the little place his mother-in-law rented him, where Hatillo leaves off and the empty fields begin, full of haze in the summer, green and flowering at the beginning of winter.

But what everyone agrees on is that the story began like this: That morning, Faust was completely fed up. His wife had threatened to make him a soup out of boots, slippers, moccasins, topsiders, whatever, since for more than a week now his customers hadn't even come in to pick up their things. Should he read the newspaper? For what? Listen to the radio? It makes me hungry. Read the Bible? Even worse. Scratch myself? It makes me nervous, and besides it messes up my skin. Faust was mulling over these things when he heard the stranger's voice for the first time: "May I, *patrón*?" It was a melodious voice, mocking and soft, like a flute. He didn't answer, and the first thing he looked at was the man's feet: "Damn!" he thought. "Sandals!" And this was the time of day when Margarita would be hoping he'd send her a little money to buy meat and vegetables or else to pay for the electricity that had been turned off. Without asking if he could come in, without even waiting for Faust's response, the stranger said to him, "A million pesos for your thoughts." Just like that, suddenly, Faust realized that this man, with his vague coloring, long toes, carefully manicured hands, and curly hair, was reading his mind as if his head were made of some sort of gelatin that let his thoughts show through. "Tell me, *patrón*," the voice now had a metallic sound, like the whistle of a knife cutting a hair. "Do you repair shoes here?" "Obviously, friend," Faust dared to say, thinking that at that very moment Margarita would be putting on the water for him and sending that little girl to the shop to see if he had gotten any money, and the noisy little brat would never stop staring at the shoes, as if nosing around, as if biding time . . .

The man said to him then, clearly, in a jeering tone, "Obviously, obviously, obviously! Everyone thinks it's obvious, and they don't even know what the word means. For example, it's obvious that the little girl will be coming now and that you don't have anything to give her." Faust thought he wasn't hearing it right, but he got hold of his astonishment and said, "What little girl?" To which the individual responded, "What little girl? Ah!" using the voice he had started with, but with a mocking expression on his face and showing him his right foot, where a small strap on his sandal had broken. "How much would it be? Do I have to take off my sandal before the little girl gets here or what?" Faust thought he was standing face to face with a madman: his skin the color of white parchment, his hands, his voice changing back and forth, his elongated feet, that shirt resembling wool, and those gray corduroy pants that no one ever wears anymore. He thought, too, that perhaps he had been smelling thinner for too long, or that, without meaning to, he had been sniffing the benzine he used to clean his fingers with, or that he was hungry, or anything else.

Up to that point he seemed to remember everything clearly,

but later everything got sort of foggy, no lie, as if obscured by the vapors that rise from the asphalt after rain. For sure, I must not have had enough coffee this morning, and now I'm seeing visions right before my very eyes, he told himself. And months later: No, it wasn't fog, it was as if he had been shaken up until the dust had blown off him like a fine talcum powder, almost transparent. Like this, like that, like something else, standing before the admiring eyes of some friends in the Chinaman's bar, no, it was in the Cubans' restaurant, in Marlene's soda, in the *pulpería* where . . .

That was when the man almost sent him spinning: "Do you believe in God?" That's all I need, Faust told himself, he doesn't see the sign. But he responded, "Protestant propaganda is prohibited on these premises." "Ah, ah, ah," said the little man, who at this point in the conversation had taken off his sandal and handed it over, demanding, "Fix this for me, if you want to earn any money." Faust picked it up to get a closer look. What kind of leather was this? Sheep. Lamb. Deerskin, maybe? What could this leather have come from?—it was such fine stuff. And he looked at the naked foot: a nearly perfect foot except for those three hairs sprouting out almost from the heel. But he didn't pay them any mind.

"Do you believe everything they tell you, about the existence of God and his son Jesus Christ and all that . . . ? If you do believe, don't say anything. But if you have any doubts, tell me!" This was said in that metallic voice that stayed in his head for so many months. . . . Doubts? Lots of them, but they're no one else's business. Just an ongoing argument with Margarita. Bitter struggles in which she complained about his disbelief, the stupidity of his stubborn refusal to go to mass, his scoffing remarks about the saints, his slamming the door in the astonished faces of the brothers who used to come to preach the Word . . . Good News? Don't make me laugh, Margarita. Don't you see that when it comes to the business of churches, there is nothing new at all? And that goes for the ones here as well as the rest? They misuse Sonny Boy's words just to make money. Don't you hear the announcements, don't you read the papers, or watch the pictures on the TV?

As if they were reading each other's minds, the stranger responded, "Doubts, well, we all have a lot of doubts, but we don't have the opportunity to analyze them. Who created the world? How does it keep turning? Who created man? Who sustains him? Who eliminates him, and who provides him with food to eat?"

"God does," Faust said, timidly.

The sound of the little man's guffaws were heard as far away as the mountains of Alajuelita, though managing to avoid touching the Cross, which showed the obvious piety of the people. "God does? Then who is it that keeps you here? Why don't they come to pick up their shoes? Why is it that Margarita is waiting before she sends the little girl here so you won't get angry? Why do you still owe on your electric bill, and why haven't you paid your rent for the last four months? You idiot! You're living with your head in the clouds amidst your clippings telling you what's happening out there, and you considereth not the beam that is in thine own eye!"

He was certain that the stranger never opened his mouth while saying all this. It was like communicating head to head, like in the movies, like when Margarita knew a customer had arrived to pick up his shoes, like when . . . The man was definitely not speaking, and yet he continued to say things, mind to mind.

"How is it that you are so stupid? And the rich people, like your neighbors who won in the lottery? And didn't that guy get rich overnight? How about the others: the old woman who won on "Wheel of Fortune"? Fifteen million, to divide between her and her children. Didn't she by chance live right here in Alajuelita?"

All right, all right, Faust said to himself, feeling this interference in his brain. But he could not fix the strap. His hands weren't working, or at least something was happening to him, as if he were having a strange dream, like when music from the neighbors' houses would reach him, then the voices, in pieces, out of sync: the music from one side and the words from the other.

"You see, now? I got right to the center of your thoughts," he said now with a new voice, full of joy, delighted and ironic; perhaps it was his true voice, to give it once more the intonation of the first one: "Do you want money? To leave this poverty behind? To go and live in Rohmoser, or in Lomas de Ayarco? To travel? To go to the Union Club? What is it you want? To have a baby with Margarita? Help your mother? send your nieces to study in the United States? Spend the summer in Miami? What do you want?"

All of it! Faust heard himself say out loud, but it was as if it weren't his voice at all, but someone else's deep inside him who was responding to this strange man with the one bare foot, with those three strange hairs that reminded him of something but he didn't know what.

"Aha! You want it all! That's what they all say. Quick and brazen. Twenty minutes ago you weren't thinking about any of this, but now you talk and talk, as if someone had given you a belt of guava juice with vodka, what you like best!" He even knows that, Faust said to himself, trying with his right hand to reach the benzine bottle so he could take a sniff or two and clear his head.

At this point in the conversation, Faust was something like a man divided: the conversation bothered him, but what the man was saying had him under a spell. He wanted him to leave. But he also wanted to get that strap fixed so he could earn a little something, even if it was next to nothing, and have a bit to send Margarita when the little girl came— although she still wasn't anywhere to be seen. The conversation, half words, half waves, went on for about ten minutes in the same tone: about the existence of God, Faust's faith, the injustices of the world, the lack of money, poverty, the rise in the price of bread, electricity, the rent laws (how much will the old woman raise the rent on me for this place?), the tropical hurricane that took a detour through Nicaragua, the skin color of blacks, the death of Christina Onassis, abortion, and all the world's plagues—until, exasperated, Faust said, "All right, then, what do you want?"

The little man responded in a laconic, almost metallic way, "Me? I don't want anything. What is it you want?"

Faust didn't have to open his mouth to answer with what the other was waiting to hear. The stranger could read his mind, and that was what he did. "All of it!" And the conversation stopped right there, as if a cold wind had suddenly blown into the little shop, and this at eleven o'clock in the morning, with the sun burning the roofs of Hatillo, with the asphalt already like gum.

"I have nothing," Faust heard himself say. "Of course you do," the man said. All this without speaking: the cobbler trying to fix the strap, the stranger moving his foot back and forth with a certain nervousness, while pulling at the fabric of his pants, as if expecting something. And it was then that Faust managed to remember the discussion he had had with Margarita on Sunday: What a bitch of a life, what a frustra-

tion! Just another day off the calendar. Debts, debts, debts.
Your brother wins in the lottery, and we don't even get a dog
turd! Sonofabitch! What good does it do you, praying like
crazy all the time, lighting candles to San Judas, making
promises to Santa Clara, when we don't even have enough
money to publish them in the newspaper. What an unbearable disgrace! Every day the same old thing, every day going
by at the same pace . . . And it was when he had said all this,
though he couldn't recall it now word for word, with this little
man talking to him at a time of day when as a rule the sun
would practically drive him crazy, when it would put him to
sleep and he would need to scratch himself to know whether
he was awake, or alive, or whatever . . . But he knew that it
was already too late to go back along the same path . . . And
that was when he said, almost tamely, "All right, let's do what
you want . . . "

"What do you mean—*let's* do it! You're the one who has
to decide, not me." OK, I've decided, then, but I'm not very
convinced about what I'm doing. You're taking advantage of
the fact that I'm nearly half asleep, that I'm all mixed up,
Faust said to himself, while his hands worked hard to fix the
strap. Which suddenly was all finished.

Then the little man tried on the sandal. "Marvelous! Just
like new!" he said. And taking out a five-hundred-peso bill,
he asked, "What do I owe you?" Faust stared at the bill; he
was disconsolate. "I don't have any change," he murmured.
"Well, all right, let it go, then. Cheap things often turn out to
be more expensive in the long run. If I had to buy one sandal
by itself it would cost me a thousand pesos, but they don't sell
them one at a time, it's fifteen hundred, made to order . . ."
and with a brightness in his voice, he added as he went out,
"Ciao, *patrón!* I hope you make the most of our deal!"

At that very moment the little girl arrived highly agitated, wearing the miniskirt that made him feel so weird and uncomfortable. "Doña Margarita wants to know if you got anything yet. She said she was looking out the window toward the mountains and suddenly something whispered to her that you were gonna be getting paid." Faust said nothing and sent her to La Peseta next door to get change for the bill, along with a pack of cigarettes and some mints.

It is well known that when she returned he bought himself an instant lottery ticket at the mercado and almost fell over when he finished scratching it off: 2,000,000 pesos. Two million, two million, TWO MILLION pesos!!! They had to sit him down at Lolo Mora's and bring him some linseed oil with *mozote* to settle him down.

Up to this point, everyone knows the story. In Hatillo, around Sagrada Familia, and even almost as far as San Felipe in Alajuelita. They were no longer poor. But Faust began acting pretty strange because he didn't want to work anymore, and Margarita became rather nervous, and they bought a house around Eighth Street, it had two stories, and Margarita put in a little shop on the ground floor. But no one would buy anything from them because of the story that had gone around, and they even fought with her sister and brother-in-law. They didn't have any children, they moved to Guadalupe, and then back to Hatillo, because Margarita was afraid to be alone in the huge house there. Faust opened another shoe repair, but it didn't catch on, and later he had to be moved out while the roof was being fixed, but he came back, and that's the way it is now; every time that doña Agripina, doña Zoraida, and the little girl Betty see a stranger who's sort of pale—no, no: fair-skinned, or dark-skinned—no, no: whose color is like that of a figurine fresh out of the kiln: light-colored—and tall, wearing sandals, rather slim, with high shoes . . . then they make the sign of the cross, turn toward the sign that reads WE ARE CATHOLIC—NO PROTESTANT PROPAGANDA allowed, and shut themselves up inside their houses, putting themselves in the hands of San Judas, Santa Clara, the Prayer of the Great Power, the Five Celestial Potencies—of God, my child, GOD!—because you don't fool around with these things. If you don't think so, just remember the case of Faust and Margarita, the ones who used to live over near Second Street, child, and now they're living in Bello Horizonte, so it is said . . .

Translated by Leland H. Chambers

Mystery Stone

Rima de Vallbona

*For Cocó, Ligia, Miguel, and those
who lovingly welcomed me
into their magic corner of Liberia*

"LADIES AND GENTLEMEN, we are now entering the
province of Guanacaste, land of wonders, as you yourselves
will see along the way. This region of the country became
part of Costa Rica by its own choice, about one hundred and
sixty-five years ago. Welcome!"

While the guide went on talking, I let myself be taken over
by the enchanting green of the passionate countryside going
by outside the bus window like images in a magic lantern.

"The name of this province comes from the huge tree
native to this region, whose flattened pods coil around like
ears, which was the reason it was called *quauhnacaztli*, from
the Nahuatl words *quauitl*, for tree, and *nacaztli*, for ear. This
area was once occupied by Aztecs and other tribes from Chi-
apas and the Caribbean."

I closed my eyes, possessed by an indefinable pleasure, and
began to imagine the *yulios*, or spirit-hearts, a kind of alter
ego that escapes through the mouths of the Chorotegas when
they die. I pictured urns filled with ashes of dead caciques
buried in the thresholds of their own homes; for a while I

73

pondered the similarities between certain duties of Catholic priests and those of indigenous priests. It's true that the latter performed animal and human sacrifices, but they also practiced celibacy, and part of their work was to teach the rituals and doctrines related to their gods; they even heard private confessions and gave out penances for sins.

"These beautiful trees on the right, the ones that have aerial roots and look like gigantic bright green parasols, are *higuerones*, or *matapalos*, of the genus *Ficus*. The tree is a strangler, because its seeds, disseminated in bird feces, germinate on another tree—of any species—and begin to grow on top of it, enveloping it and choking it until it finally replaces it. A charlatan tree, but one of incomparable beauty."

It's been a long time since I've experienced such a gratifying lassitude as I feel today. It wasn't such a bad idea after all, succumbing to the irresistible invitation of my cousins Matilde, the older one, and Angelina, the baby of the family. For a few days I have left behind my inviolable solitude in Escazú, where for so many years I have gone out only to do the daily shopping.

"During the dry season, the countryside here turns completely yellow. It's autumn relocated to the heat of the tropics, because the yellow tree bark, without foliage, is covered with flowers. When they fall, they paint the ground an intense yellow, which then blends with the old gold color of the hay turning yellow beneath the endless sun.

"There, on your right, rising from the immense plain of Guanacaste, is the Cordillera de Tilarán, where you'll find the volcano Arenal, which has the world's largest volcanic lake. Arenal was thought to be extinct, but just a short while ago it began to erupt, and lava and stones completely buried the small town built on the mountainside. It's now fully active, thundering and spewing clouds of embers and smoke that darken the sky no matter how clear the day is.

"Yes, sir, you are correct." The guide addressed one of the tourists on the bus. "The province of Guanacaste has several volcanoes. On this tour, we will visit the Rincón de la Vieja, famous because on its fifty-hectare surface are scattered The Frying Pans or The Burners, which are lagoons of bubbling mud and chasms through which vapors and gases escape. There are also clay cones and pools of boiling water.

"After we pass the city of Bagaces, we will arrive in Liberia, the White City, so called because in the past it was paved with limestone gravel, of which now barely a trace remains. But in point of fact, I must tell you this: our mothers and grandmothers recount that at night, in the moonlight, the city appeared completely white and luminous, and such was its brightness that you could read in the middle of the night without electric lights."

"Excuse me, miss, but what are those enormous balls of stone or whatever, sitting in front of some of the buildings and houses, the ones I've been seeing ever since we left San José?" another tourist asked. "Are those the ones mentioned in that book by that North American, the stones that are supposed to have been brought here by extraterrestrials because the indigenous people had neither the knowledge nor the ability to make them so round?"

"You are referring to the lithic spheres. Actually, they are a true mystery rock, perhaps granite or andesite or a sedimentary rock. They date from the years 400 to 1200 A.D. and come from the archaeological zone of Diquís, near the indigenous cemeteries from which they have been removed. As you can see, some have ended up here in this province. You can find them in all sizes, from a few centimeters to more than two meters in diameter, and weighing up to sixteen tons. In *The Summary of the Natural History of the Indies*, Fernández de Oviedo, the first official chronicler of the Spanish empire, mentioned that in one valley in Cuba about fifteen kilometers long, they are found in great abundance, in many sizes and so perfectly round that they don't seem to have been made by human hands. It's believed that they are symbols of the sun or the moon, and that those who possessed them in pre-Columbian times were probably noted for their advanced political and religious standing. This last notion, however, is only conjecture."

Upon arriving in Liberia, according to the agreement I had made with the travel agency, I went to stay with my cousins. I would have preferred to stay in a hotel; my timidity, lack of social graces, and many years out of touch with my relatives inclined me to justify lodging with the tourist group. But my cousins, with a thousand compliments and displays of affection, insisted otherwise, and I couldn't refuse.

The moment I set foot in the bedroom they gave me, I entered into a magic world, in which a certain something lingered in the air; the enchantment was enhanced by the vases of *huelenoches* that sat on the chest of drawers, the chirping of the cicadas, the whisper of the leaves fluttering in the breeze, and the excited trill of the birds. A strange drowsiness came over me and enhanced the smells wafting in through the open window: emanations of wild plants, flowers, and ripe mangoes, which, in the July heat, released aromatic juices while they rotted in the dust of the path, generously shaded by trees.

Little by little, inadvertently, I let myself be taken over by lethargy. . . . Just when a peaceful rest relaxed my nerves and muscles, disaster struck: gigantic lithic spheres began to roll around in my dreams. And as if this weren't bad enough, other smaller ones, the size of tennis balls but made of solid granite, began to rain down from the sky. All of them, large and small, grazed me, struck me, crushed me, but none of them hurt me because my *yulio* was outside my exhausted body, contemplating the disaster from high up on the wall.

Extremely distressed and drenched with sweat, I awoke to the sound of the alarm clock. In a single gulp I drank the water in the pitcher that sat next to the head of the bed and got ready to go out.

After a short visit to the city and a frugal dinner, my cousins and I engaged in an after-dinner conversation that revolved around indigenous art and ceramics. Matilde showed me how the ancestral knowledge in her fingers enabled her to repair pieces destroyed by grave robbers' greed for gold. She told me that she had petitioned the Ministry of Culture to open a regional archaeological museum in Liberia. In reply, however, two guards arrived to confiscate all the indigenous pieces that she had been using to teach high-school students to appreciate indigenous art.

"They took everything, not to exhibit the pieces and educate the public, like I had intended, but to warehouse it all up in who knows which forgotten corner of the Bellavista Museum in San José. We were left staring at the wall. They carted away absolutely everything except for this lithic sphere, and only because they didn't notice it." From behind a flowerpot, where a leafy palm shimmered, she retrieved a ball of granite the size of a cannonball. "Look, Berta, what strange contortions it makes when you start it rolling!"

As a matter of fact, it turned on its own axis, like a top, and at the same time it moved around the room in unexpected circles and spirals. It stopped for a few moments, then suddenly, without being touched, came to life again, as if through its own force and will.

"When it stops, it gives the impression of having eyes and a mouth, and it seems to look at you from another world," Angelina commented, and she was right, because I had the same experience, so much so that a slight shiver passed through my body every time the sphere stopped to begin again. Probably the result of my afternoon nightmare, I thought, and exhaustion from my long trip.

Juana, the cook, who came in to clear the table, shook her head in disapproval when she saw us handling the ball.

"You shouldn't play with that," she warned us. "When I clean the house, doña Matilde knows that I never touch that ball. They say there's a spirit shut up inside, and it always knows when someone's going to die. No one knows how it knows, but the stone comes to rest upon them during the night and then the victim kicks the bucket."

Matilde, Angelina, and I exchanged a mocking "don't-bother-us-who-know-everything-with-those-ignorant-bare-foot-peasant-superstitions" glance. Without noticing and with the charming naiveté that characterizes the people of my country, Juana continued to relate stories like the one about the woman who was found dead, hugging the sphere, the same sphere that was now rolling on the floor in front of us. Afraid of it, the dead woman's relatives wanted to bury the stone ball so that it would rest in the depths of the earth, but Matilde wanted to keep it and add it to her collection. According to Juana, as soon as the sphere came into the house, there were hints of bad omens, because that was when the authorities came to confiscate the rest of the indigenous pieces.

"Believe me, I have a lot of respect for this sad little stone head that's bumping around on the floor right now. A lot of respect! It's silly, they say around here, but you never know. Look at those little eyes, look how they watch you! Anyone can see how sad they are. And it's you, doña Berta, it's you they're watching." She addressed me in a mournful tone, a mixture of fear and surprise in her voice, as if at that very moment she had heard the prophecy of some Chorotega divinity, one who had branded me as its proprietary victim.

"Eyes? You see eyes on that ball?" Matilde asked in a teasing voice.

I saw them, just as Juana did, and I think Angelina did, too, judging by what she'd said before. And truly, no matter where its movements took it, the sphere kept its eyes fixed on me, on me alone, every time it stopped. The air in the room seemed thick, suffocating, like a true nightmare. I wanted to cry out, to flee, but my timidity, my habit of keeping silent, perhaps fear as well, all kept me frozen. I wanted to ask Juana why, since she seemed to possess the secret, but I couldn't get a single word out, my tongue was heavy, my body felt half asleep. In the midst of the July heat, I broke into a cold sweat, and an intense pain in my chest caused me to retire early.

I wanted never to forget those happy moments, so before I went to bed I recorded my impressions of the trip and of all the affection—to which I am so unaccustomed—that Matilde and Angelina had showed me.

I am so happy here that I never want to go back to my corner in Escazú. I will go back, because I have no choice, but my yulio *will stay here, enjoying itself, enveloped in the aroma of the* huele-noches, *which have just begun to release their nocturnal perfume into my room. But . . . what's that I hear? I can still hear the echo that the lithic sphere makes on the tile when it rolls around . . . Yes, it's rolling, I hear it clearly over all the sounds of the night. It's the ball, the ancestral mystery stone . . . It's coming closer to my bedroom. Will my afternoon nightmare continue? It can't be. Unbelievable. More than unbelievable, monstrously absurd!*

That was the end of the notes that my cousin Berta had made in a meticulous diary during her visit to our city. The rest? The rest remains a mystery. Dawn found Berta in bed, lifeless, with the lithic sphere, the mystery stone that had so intrigued her the night before, clutched to her breast. How had the sphere ended up in her bed? Had she herself brought it? Last night, when I turned out the lights, I closed the door to the room where the sphere was kept. I'm sure I did.

The coroner informed us that the autopsy showed it had been a massive heart attack, at approximately midnight.

I disagree completely. I'd like to let him know the truth, that she died of loneliness. The doctors and other authorities in Liberia didn't know that Berta—orphaned in infancy, a single woman always closed up in her house in Escazú, without friends, timid, afraid of the world, even of us, the cousins who grew up playing with her—wanted to die here, immersed in the love and affection we had extended to her since she arrived yesterday morning. "I'm terrified to go back home, I'm afraid I'll die there alone, that no one will find my body for days, and when they do, it will be rotten. I'm afraid of my loneliness. I would give anything to die here, to leave my *yulio* here, where everything is warmth and tenderness, in the magic of Guanacaste's natural splendor," she confessed to me when I asked her if she'd like to spend a few more days with us. Yes, she died from intense loneliness, and her embrace of the stone sphere is testimony to the lack of affection she lived with: her heart, starved of love, could not tolerate the dose we had been administering since yesterday.

Translated by Barbara Paschke

The Bongo

Carlos Salazar Herrera

"Hey, bongo man, where're you going?"
"To the Jicaral salt mines!"
"You don't have any room for me, do you?"
"Why not, my friend, come on!"

A BONGO! A little boat that's just like a story.

A bongo is a small sailboat that holds only a few people. The hull is made from a single piece hewn from the trunk of a big cashew tree, blow by blow, with ax and adze.

A bongo is made for calm waters.

A bongo cannot venture into open ocean, like the big ships that hold many people and move many things on their long voyages.

A bongo cannot lose sight of land because, despite everything, it is still a tree. The colors of the setting sun paint the sails fore and aft; and at night, mast and spanker boom, gaff and beam trace out new patterns in the stars.

The bongo man was a kind old soul in his sixties. Outside, as solid as a keel. Inside, as transparent as a sail.

He serviced the coast in the Gulf of Nicoya.

Pitahaya, Jicaral, Lepanto, Chomes, and Paquera. Salt, sand, charcoal, bananas, mangrove, coconuts, and tamarind.

To be charitable, he had taken in a little girl who'd been

left alone when her mother, a distant relative of his, had died. From then on he had dedicated himself to taking care of his two loves: the bongo and his adopted daughter, Natalia, who always accompanied him on his voyages.

"And where is Natalia?" I asked him.

The bongo man lowered his head in enormous sorrow, and he seemed to be pushing grief back with his hand.

"She drowned. She drowned on me here, in this very gulf. Not long ago . . . It was my fault. You've seen how I've suffered!"

Let's see what happened to the bongo man:

One day at high tide, around dawn, the bongo man weighed anchor and, in a northeasterly wind, struck out toward Puntarenas.

It was a bad day. In the vicinity of Chomes a calm locked him in, and for several hours he was at the mercy of the current. The bongo man went to the rudder and Natalia went to the bench at the prow. A load of *currarés* lay between them.

There was nothing to do but wait.

The bongo man had noticed that Natalia . . . she wasn't a worthless brat anymore. He had noticed how modestly the girl pulled down her skirt every time a southern breeze uncovered her thighs, and beneath the sails he had mused . . . how the limes were ripening on the tree!

That day, taking advantage of the calm, he told her:

"Natalia, you're not a child anymore, and—I'm not that old. I took you in, I've watched over you, and I've loved you a lot. I've thought, um—I've come to think that if you're grateful and—if you love me a little, well, Father Raimundo told me there's really nothing in the way of our getting married and . . ."

"I don't want to—I can't, Daddy!" she interrupted. "I love you—but in another way. I'm grateful to you, but . . . "

"Natalia, there is no *but!*" the bongo man shouted, his mood changing. "I've taken care of you, and I've already arranged everything. Tomorrow you're going with me to the church. Oh! And—and don't call me Daddy! Understand?"

Nothing more was said about the matter.

The bongo man dropped anchor in a deep spot and, waiting, waiting for favorable winds, went to sleep on the bench at the stern.

When he woke up, Natalia wasn't in the bongo.

He spent the rest of the day and night searching the dark gulf.

"Natalia! . . . My little darling!"

And he never saw her again.

A black seabird, high in the sky, hung motionless for a long time, like an anchor suspended in space. Then, sounding the vast immensity of the sky, it made a stylized descent.

The bongo man looked at me and said:

"Sometimes the water leaps up, like now—you know?—and gets on your face, and you don't know if you're crying, because—sea and tears are both salt water."

"Tell me," I asked the bongo man. "And Natalia—did she know how to swim?"

"Like a fish."

"And tell me, didn't she have a boyfriend?"

"No, not that I know of . . . Sometimes I'd see her with Jacobo, a good boy who used to help me load the bongo."

"And where is Jacobo?"

"Back then he told me he was going to work at Punta Quepos, and he disappeared without a word."

He paused to reflect a moment, and then his eyes opened wide, and with a new tone in his voice, he added: "Man!—I hadn't thought about that!" And then, smiling sweetly, with his face spattered by the sea—or by tears—he said, "Well, so be it—may God bless her."

In the heart of the Gulf of Nicoya a pelican dropped beak first and came back up with a corvina. Another pelican, flying just above the water, snatched the fish and fled toward the mangroves.

Translated by James Hoggard

She Wore a Bikini

Alfonso Chase

IT WAS THE EIGHTEENTH OF AUGUST at exactly nine o'clock in the morning. I did see her, for sure. But it was just as if I hadn't. Everyone knows about the Adelita González affair because it came out in the newspapers and for several weeks everyone was talking about the case. No one knows whether Adelita González ever returned or not, but the fact is that she never went home and her family ended up selling her things, and little by little all her friends have gradually forgotten about her. I knew her because she demonstrated beauty products, and she used to like to go to art shows, and she and I shared a great admiration for Maria Callas, whom she actually resembled, according to what her closest friends say. But it seems to me that her style was more like Renata Tebaldi's.

Adelita González was from a very good family. She came from the people who made this country, and she ended up selling beauty products when she no longer wanted to go on applying her creams to her own face, which had started to wrinkle a little. She was an expert with makeup, capable of transforming La Segua into Daniela Romo and Elizabeth Taylor into Morticia.

I think she had studied in New York, or else Paris—at least that's what I heard her say. She was from such a good family that she never lacked for a clientele, and getting your makeup from Adelita González was not only very expensive but in fact an honor. She lived alone. In a huge house left to her by her sisters, who had become nuns and lived in Nicaragua, or maybe it was Guatemala, since occasionally she would get herself a ticket and disappear there somewhere. She liked to travel. When she was a little girl she'd been sent to visit some aunts in the States, and she ended up with an itch to travel. So once a year she would go off to Europe, to Mexico, maybe Peru, and this year she had been wanting to go to Japan. Or to Australia, according to what she told us at the last show we saw her at. There's been a lot of talk about Adelita González's trips, but I think it's just talk. Someone once said that when she was abroad in those countries she would be transformed: she would stop being the Adelita we all knew and would turn herself into a completely different woman, not just in her makeup but in her clothing too and even in the way she talked.

When LACSA made the first direct flights to New York, Adelita was one of the first passengers to get off and breathe the air of that huge airport; it was polluted, of course, but at least it wasn't the foul smell of tacos and deep-fried food that we're used to around here. So it hasn't seemed so strange to me that she just disappeared and dropped out of sight ever since the eighteenth of August.

But the truth is that Adelita González is needed around here. I always liked to have long talks with her because she knew all the stories about everyone in San José. While going about the business of face creams and makeup, one learns a

great deal, as I was able to observe. During these transforma-
tions women's tongues loosen, and Adelita—with astonishment written on her face—would hear things that not even
the OIJ knows. It was something people mentioned often
when she disappeared. Because many women, and even their
husbands, used to ask her for hints about what she had been
told in so-and-so's house that could be useful at what's-her-
name's and later on at you-know-who's. By this I'm not trying
to say that Adelita González was gossipy and still less that
she would repeat in conversation what she had heard in those
homes. But occasionally her tongue would come untied and,
without giving names, of course, she would tell things that
would make your hair stand on end, and then she'd leave us
up in the air, like a suspense novel, until the next week, when
she would continue the story with what she had heard in the
latest makeup session. They say that many people were after
Adelita González to ask her things that only she would know,
and that when the Iran-Contra thing hit, Adelita knew all
about the situation down to the last detail, even down to
the names of the politicians here who were being supported
by Contra funds. One of the most charming things about
Adelita was the way she would tell a story. She must have
had a gift for it, since she gave everything a touch of suspense
without giving away any names, but we all knew who she was
talking about, just by paying a little attention.

It was by sheer accident that I saw her on August eighteenth. I was in Yaohan's, waiting for some friends, when I
saw her coming out carrying a bag and some books she had
bought nearby, and after saying hello she said she was going
to tan herself completely black because she was on the way to
the beach to get rid of her stress. A kiss on the cheek and she
was gone, who knows where. There's been a lot of specula-

tion about what happened since then, above all after we were
called to testify.

She left her car at a cousin's, one of the Gonzálezes of
Escazú, driving it herself up to the garage, and from then
on no one knows a thing. How did she get to the Coca Cola
station to catch the bus? Why didn't she go to the beach in
her car, or at least, in the minibus run by the tour company?
Or better yet, by plane, to save time? These questions are all
nothing more than speculation, since the thing is that she
went by bus, one of those that run between San José and
Quepos, and that the other passengers recognized her from
the photo they were shown. They said she was reading at
first and afterward she started talking with everyone; and
right around Orotina she got off the bus to buy some fruit
and stretch her legs. After this she went on with the trip,
asking someone something about where Kilometer 35 was, or
33, somewhat concerned that no one could tell her exactly.
She was wearing white slacks and flats (color unknown) and
carried a small satchel. She didn't get off near Jacó but about
two kilometers before it, where someone (without being
absolutely sure about it) showed her where Kilometer 35 was.
The strange thing is that a man was waiting there for Adelita
González: a young guy, good-looking, about twenty-eight, so
the passengers said, who was signaling to her from the top of
a small hill. Adelita said good-bye to everyone and told them
she would probably see them again that weekend in Quepos,
where she'd be going next. No one knows anything about the
man waiting for her, because she registered alone at the hotel
at 2:40 in the afternoon, giving her real name and asking for
a public telephone even before her room was ready. No one
knows what Adelita González said at the time, nor whom she
spoke with, but a woman who worked in the hotel said that

she looked mad, as if she were talking with someone who exasperated her. But nothing more. The young man at the desk said afterward that she had requested a room away from the noise of the discotheque, and that all the calls she made were made from the public phone, and that she didn't receive any. Before going down to the beach—it was rather cloudy that day—she went up to the restaurant to have a piña colada, and greeted some women there, wives of some travel agents who surely must have been among her clients but who later on didn't want to testify, feigning ignorance.

Something else we liked about Adelita González was that she showed good taste in everything. Her bathing suit, according to the hotel gardener, was nothing special—it was just like the ones worn by all the young women her age—but he did notice that she had a radio, or rather a walkie-talkie, as if to complicate things. No one besides the gardener saw her with the device. And later he forgot everything. Her good taste was reflected in all her things, but especially in her perfumes, about which she was—if you can put it this way—a fanatic. Nothing that had been made here. Pure Bruno Pitti or Estée Lauder, but brought from Paris or London. Cigarettes, when she smoked, only Benson & Hedges; and a touch of Rémy Martin, to vary the afternoons on the ground floor of the Hotel Costa Rica, where she used to sit, waiting for nighttime. All this comes to mind because so many people were struck by the fragrance of her perfume, which remained for along time in the room from which Adelita González had by then disappeared after spending three days and four nights in the hotel, though it grew much fainter at dawn, as far as they were able to determine, since she never came down for breakfast.

No one knows what became of Adelita González. For

two days they searched for her in the ocean. Up and down the beach, almost to Doña Ana. But nothing. Beside a small waterfall they found a pack of cigarettes: Benson & Hedges, and close to some nearby rocks, a broken mirror, a small one like the ones that come in a compact. Adelita González must have been walking around there and farther down the beach to be able to disappear that way. No death notice has come out because the family isn't certain whether she has been drowned, kidnapped, or murdered, since her body has never appeared. It seems that she spent all those days writing in a notebook that has never been found, or else calling on the public telephone as well as doing some other little things, now consigned to oblivion, that might have clarified the situation a little. I have no definite opinions about the case, but I have gotten into investigating it, not really deeply, but at least out of respect for my friendship with her: the victim, the deceased, the missing, the vanished—however one might think of Adelita González now. Her hairdresser, Melito, ventured the theory that it's possible, since she was bored with everything and everyone, that she may have decided to have some plastic surgery (she needed it anyway) and to change her hairstyle, to be what she really wanted to be, which Melito never bothered to specify. The hypothesis doesn't sound so strange, especially concerning Adelita. But it doesn't jibe with her going to the beach, the walkie-talkie, the notebook, the phone calls, getting off the bus before arriving at the hotel entrance, meeting the man in the red shirt right alongside the road, and not even with the little mirror found among the rocks on the beach.

Several depositions about the case may be taken into consideration, which, because of their contradictions, retain some interest.

THE BUSDRIVER

She got on at the Coca Cola station. She sat in one of the seats in the back and started to read while the bus was loading. Once on the highway, she kept looking out the window, as if trying to see if any cars were following. I could see her face, and her hair, and I was even going to try to get her attention, but only for a few seconds on three or four occasions. When we passed the airport, the woman—at that age you never know if they are señoritas or not—moved forward a few seats to ask some girls if they knew where Kilometer 33 was: I could hear it clearly. Even though I've been on this route for five years, I didn't know anything about any Kilometer 33, but later I discovered that it was where an old milestone marked a pasture where they say airplanes have been seen at two o'clock in the morning. No, not seen—heard, really. Then I heard her asking again, and the whole way after Orotina she sat near the rear window, to keep looking at the road. Someone said Kilometer 35, or 33, was coming up, and she rang the bell. Then I could see a man on top of a little knoll, he was wearing shorts, a flowery shirt, and tennis shoes, but nothing else. I never thought any more about it until I saw the photo in *La Extra* and began to put things together.

THE HOTEL RECEPTIONIST

She came in and registered with her name: Adelita González. I didn't see anything strange about her. Only I did notice the smell of her perfume and the fact that she immediately asked for the public phone. But it was all normal. We don't usually notice details about our guests, since we see so many and we don't like to dig into what they come here to do. We assume that they come to relax, but it doesn't matter to us what happens to them outside the hotel. She was just a woman, like all the others. They come here all the time. Especially the wives of travel agents, or gringas or Germans, they are the ones we see the most. But she was from here. It couldn't be anybody other than the one I saw later in the newspaper. She took the key and never brought it back. I gave her a room that's like a little cottage, close to the one occupied by the boys who come here to surf. Yes, I saw her a lot, calling on the phone and poking around in the local crafts shop. Nothing the other people don't do. I never saw her in a bathing suit, or in a bikini, like the women from the little snack stand down there say they saw her in. She was too old to wear a tanga, the way the laborers at the cabins at the end of the beach said, much less dental floss, like it came out in the newspaper. She didn't have black hair, either, like it said in *La Extra*. She was a blonde, tending toward red. Dyed, of course. You have to be careful about things like this, that you don't confuse the woman—excuse me, the señorita—with a tourist from Panama who did have black hair and went around all day in a tanga . . .

THE CLEANING WOMAN

I saw her when we met in the corridor, since I was coming from doing the cleaning in her cottage. Her hair was a kind of chestnut brown, and she was wearing some white slacks and carried a satchel and a bigger suitcase. Nothing strange about that. I really liked her perfume, it was like violets; well, perfumes fade away very quickly here. She went in and shut the door and then opened it again to give me a little bag of *chicharrones*, fried pork rinds. I took them just to be polite, because I never eat those things, I'm a vegetarian.

Later on, along about five, she was walking through the bar as if she was expecting someone, and then she went to make a call from the phone, the public telephone that's in front of the reception desk. When it was almost dark she went out to walk along the beach, with a little plastic beachbag and a scarf, a pretty one, thrown over her shoulders. Then I lost sight of her until the next day, in the morning. She was going down to the beach wearing a two-piece bathing suit, not a tanga or a bikini, like all the gossips around here are saying, and carrying a magazine and a notebook. Then she disappeared toward the west, where the waterfall and the rocks are. It seemed to me she was talking with someone, someone who was near the bus stop, but I couldn't be sure about that. I never saw her again until they started making all the fuss about her and went to look for her in her room, where I'd been doing the cleaning every day at about ten in the morning, and the only thing I noticed was the fragrance of her perfume and a cassette player, a tiny one on the nightstand that was taken away by the police or the family. I had been fooling around with it, so they must have found my fingerprints on it. But nothing else. No, I never saw her go in the water, at least not in front of the hotel. I can't confirm what those laborers say, that they saw her in the water almost at the end of the beach . . .

A LABORER

We saw her going in the water down where the UNEBANCO cottages are. Wow, what a woman! What a shape! Wearing just a little bitty piece of dental floss and something that from a distance looked like a little line drawn across her breasts. First she would put one foot in, and then the other. And then she would run into the waves with such swaying and jiggling that it took our breath away. That's the way it was every day, early in the morning and then just before nightfall. Since she couldn't see us, we spent the days doing our work and watch-

ing her. After getting wet in the ocean, she would throw herself on the sand, turning over now and then to get the sun,
and stopping just in time to keep from getting burned. Then
she would put some cream on and rub herself all over; she'd
look all around again and put on some oil, or whatever it was,
on the places I was telling you about. The construction job
nearly collapsed right there. Or we nearly fell off the roof. She
spent a long time at this, but I don't know how long exactly.
I noticed that she would take a black thing, something like a
walkie-talkie, out of her plastic beachbag and start talking to
someone, but I can't say for sure that's what it was. We never
saw her with anyone, and those books, they were just for
show, because she never read a thing during that time. Then
she would get up, throw a towel over her shoulders, and start
to walk down the beach, barefoot. We had already started
home, thinking just what you're thinking. And that's what we
know—excuse me, what I know. Now you can ask the others,
just in case . . .

THE GOSSIPS AT THE FOOD STAND

We've been working here for something like twenty years,
selling lunch things. It was don Victoriano who recommended
us, and here we stayed. We can state that we saw her every
day. Ever since she came down the highway, on foot, because
at that time, after lunch, we're in the habit of sitting in the
patio, listening to the radio. She was very pretty, and quite
young, considering how old they say she was on the TV. She
had a satchel and two suitcases, one big one and one small,
and some magazines and some books. She would come out
in the mornings and afternoons, and then she would come
out again almost at nightfall. Nothing out of this world, considering the women who come to the hotel. You never even

know who they are, but they are all tall and blonde. But she was kind of brown-haired and not so tall, though taller than us. Some of them come here looking for a boyfriend. It's not nice to say so, but we have seen things that if we hadn't turned our eyes away in time we'd have already been damned to hell. Nothing out of this world, but here people go crazy with just the smell of the ocean. Ladies stop being ladies. Men behave like little kids, and the surfer boys are always ready to go on a spree, and sometimes they even go swimming in the raw, not around here, of course, but down where we go to get our firewood.

She would come out in a two-piece bathing suit, but then she would take it off and be almost the way God brought her into this world. A minibikini, or a teensy little tanga, and she didn't look bad, either, she looked like a twenty-year-old, she almost looked like a completely different woman. One day she was talking with a handsome guy in shorts and tennis shoes, really muscular, like the ones who come here with their surfboards in the summer. They didn't talk long, like right there by the bridge, and he handed something to her, some kind of package, but we don't know what it was. It seemed funny to us, it really did, that some stranger could bring her something here. But nothing is strange anymore. We never saw her up close because she never came to buy anything, but Natalia, the cleaning woman from the hotel, told us that she ate breakfast alone and had dinner almost at nighttime, but that she spent the day listening to conversations on a huge cassette player that the police took away, or else the family, after everything began to come out. We don't know what happened to her. The night before it was discovered she wasn't anywhere around, there was a god–awful lightning storm, and about nine we saw something like a little light from a launch out there, or a small yacht, sending signals to the beach. But that's common around here. Because there are guests who rent boats to go off and whoop it up somewhere else, or couples who rent them for a honeymoon cruise. We have no idea what could have happened to her. Oh, yes: we insist that she wore a little bikini, but we don't remember what color it was. Now we're getting tired of all these questions about Teresita González—that was her name, wasn't it? My son sent me clippings from the papers so we could get the whole story and see the pictures they took of us when the journalists were here. Just one thing we want to get clear: she wore a bikini!

THE GARDENER

She was pretty close to where I work around the cottages, and I could watch her from the moment she arrived, despite the fact that always by two in the afternoon I leave the hotel. Nothing out of this world. I heard her talking with someone in her room, though that could have been the radio they said she brought; because it wasn't music but something like conversation. She smiled at me two or three times and she gave me a book about mental health that the investigators have been looking through: *Rest and Live*. It's a book that teaches us to live without straining, which is an art, like using the magic powers of the mind and the guide to a happy life. I like all that a lot. And she must have read my mind, because that book is worth about nine hundred pesos and I couldn't get it around here. To me she seemed like a very special woman. She was tall, well built, though a little fat for my taste, which at my age is satisfied with just looking. I saw her leave in the morning and again later in the afternoon. She must be a vegetarian, because they told me in the dining room that she only ate salads.

But she really wore a lot of makeup for someone going to the beach, and that was something that really surprised me. What really got my attention was the fact that she would change her makeup every day. No one has mentioned this, but it seems very interesting to me. She changed her face like you would change your handkerchief. One day she would go out with a lot of lipstick on her mouth. The next day she would have a tiny little mouth, and in the afternoon her eyelashes would be standing straight out, like they were artificial, which gave her a really strange look. I think she wore a wig, but I can't be sure, because she changed her hair a lot from one day to the next, too. I never saw her go in the water. There must be some confusion, because I never saw her in the ocean, not even when I went to throw the clippings away at the end of the beach. She spent her time reading. Books on mental concentration, of course, or on how to win friends, or about spiritual things, because she gave me the impression of being given to things like that. Yes, she wore a bikini, but it was a very respectable one. I don't know if it was really a bikini, but it was a lilac-colored bathing suit that went very well with her skin, which seemed healthy to me, and very young considering how old the radio said she was. I can't tell you anything else now because it's a waning moon and I've got to go and prune the shrubs. She smiled at me twice, and she had nice teeth. Nothing out of this world, although she was a beauty of a woman, and so healthy! But she never went in the water, even though she went around in a bathing suit . . .

MELITO

I've known her for about ten years. She always treated me special, particularly when she came back from one of her trips. She would send me clients, the same ones she was doing the makeup for. She was very fussy about getting her hair cut, and lately she insisted that I change her hairstyle. She spent hours and hours looking through catalogues, but she always preferred her own in the end. She liked to talk about the things that were happening in the country, especially about political scandals, contraband, drug traffic. But there was something that didn't set right with me. It was OK that she liked to travel, but sometimes it seemed to me that she had some jobs to take care of. As if she were working for someone, or something. But she was very strict in her habits and said that it was necessary to establish the death penalty for perverts and drug dealers. A friend of mine thinks she was working for the police and that they did away with her for playing detective. But that's all very strange. The people who work for Interpol and things like that are not girls from good families, and she was first cousin to half the country, with the blood she had in her veins. She would laugh at all that stuff and say that genealogies are only good for breeding cattle, as her Uncle Ricardo said.

She used to get combed out here, but she always arrived already made up. She would send me really good clients, who never made me do much unless they called me to come to their houses to comb them out. Impossible! I can't close up the salon. She wasn't gossipy, but she liked to know everything about everyone. It was almost an obsession with her, and she had an incredible eye for the messes women get into, she really liked that. She knew all the gossip about her clients, who later became her friends, but she liked to keep their little secrets.

About her very little was known. Just that she liked to travel, and once a client told me that when she was in another country she became different in every way—in her clothes, her hairstyle, down to her way of walking. Someone else told me that she had seen her in Lima with a young man, sort of muscular, but it seems strange to me because she always liked more mature men, men with the kind of elegance the Rocky-types nowadays don't have. I read the statements that appeared in the papers, but the people who saw her there are swinging their bats too high, or else they are hiding what they know. Especially the old women at the food stand. I don't think she wore a bikini. Once she brought in a photo album from one of her trips, but the pictures of her always showed her alone, in front of some big building, and there was one very nice one taken at Niagara Falls. Yes. She had two sisters who were nuns. Once a woman told me that she had another sister, her father's doing, but that they had never even spoken to each other. Family things. Inheritances and stuff like that. Because she was very straitlaced and liked to talk with intellectuals and was a friend to artists who sometimes went to the theater with her or to the movies. I never knew about any of her sweethearts. But they say that her lifelong boyfriend used to drive her crazy, with a male friend of hers. Maybe that's why she was so strange. I knew her well, but nothing more than what I've told you. No. Juan barely knew her, because she never invited us to her house. That's the way she was. A little reserved, but friendly and even a little bit playful when she got into telling stories. But I am sure of one thing: she did not wear a bikini and she did not like cassette players. I don't know why. But I'm certain that she preferred good sound equipment and she had even bought some, the latest thing—one that plays steel disks, or whatever they're called . . .

We all know about the Adelita González affair. It all came out in the papers, and for several weeks everyone was talking about the case. I don't know what could have happened to Adelita González, really. I stopped thinking about her after six months or so. Other more important things kept me busy, and I was on the verge of forgetting about her entirely until a few weeks ago, when I received a little postcard from the Cayman Islands, and then another from New York, and finally one from Venice. No message, either handwritten or printed. But all of them bore a stamp that shows a very tall palm tree, and if you look at it closely under a glass, you can make out a woman wearing a bikini. But I'm not sure about this. It could be that I'm getting mixed up. We all know about the Adelita González affair. The one who was wearing a bikini. A tanga. Why not? The last time anyone saw her she had on this little bit of dental floss and a tiny strip you know where. It came out in the papers, but after a little while no one talked about it anymore . . .

Translated by Leland H. Chambers

The Carbonero

Carlos Salazar Herrera

AND SO, IN A COLD, grief-stricken voice, the carbonero said: "I must get revenge! . . . I'm going to think up a punishment that'll last her a lifetime, that'll torment her as long as she draws breath. I'm going to think—how to put an end to her laughter forever! That pretty laugh of hers."

Ah! . . . as she says.

It was one of those stormy nights when the fog lays shrouds on Cerro de la Muerte.

That Saturday, shivering through the chills from his fever, the carbonero walked from the work camp to his hut, taking the dark, wet shortcut through the oak grove, under the crisscross of branches, among the haphazard columns that resembled the mossy ruins of a gloomy cathedral filled with the incense of fog.

Now and then he heard the low notes and drums of Afro-Caribbean music, mixed with cheerful outbursts and voices.

His hut was at the end of the shortcut, next to the two

shacks for the mules and the charcoal; the hut was for Ibo the carbonero and his wife, Lila.

He went into the silent hut and closed the door. A few flames still played like salamanders among the cinders in the hearth.

He sat down in a dark corner, managed to calm his thoughts of revenge, and began mulling over his life. Images passed in front of him like a parade of ghosts: the first ones smiling, some somber, the last ones gloomy.

Two years back, he had married Lila, a pretty girl living with her parents in La Estrella, and he brought her to his secluded hut sunk among the oaks and fog on the unyielding, rocky slopes of Cerro de la Muerte.

And he remembered the dialogue repeated almost word for word every night:

"It's really cold, Lila!"

"Really. Did you shut the door tight, Ibo?"

"Yes. You didn't put out the fire, did you?"

"No. But I did poke it. The mules?"

"I've already taken care of them. And the charcoal stacks, too."

"Turn off the light."

"Sure. Cover up good."

"My feet are frozen stiff, Ibo."

"Then get up close to me, Lila."

"When are we getting out of here?"

"Soon. Do you love me?"

"Ah! . . . "

And time passed, but the child they longed for did not arrive and . . . each day they had less to talk about.

The carbonero had promised his wife when he married her that he would sell his property and then they would go to La Estrella, near her family, where they would set up some kind of business. But two years went by, during which, like trees that lack sprouts, they became hardened by the silence. And sometimes two years become eternal, like the Colossus of Memnon . . .

He thought about the team of mules on whose backs he loaded the sacks of blackened burlap bursting at the seams with charcoal and how the four emaciated beasts, hitched together with their ropes—tail and muzzle, tail and muzzle, tail and muzzle, bound for market—covered many leagues twice a week.

Ibo and Lila dedicated themselves to the tough job of hauling, their lives isolated and routine, without any future, lacking both tranquillity and diversion.

The chunks of oak were burned into charcoal, to be converted into a little money—hot black money—hard to come by.

Thus oppressed by the constant waves of fog, they lived with despair and with boredom. Sunk in a cold jungle covered with moss and orchids of absurd colors and forms. Tormented by a gale whose moaning sounded like the flute of the god Pan.

And so they vegetated in that huge, terrifying oak grove, without sunrises, without horizons.

One day, engineers, tractor-drivers, and crews of day laborers and woodcutters began to arrive.

They felled hundreds of trees. They made slashes, ditches, and bridges, they filled in areas. They built the Pan-American Highway and, some three hundred meters from Ibo's hut, they set up a work camp.

The carbonero was happy. Now he could haul his charcoal more easily, over a good highway, and the poor mules would come back from their journey less exhausted. It would also be easy to sell his property at a good price and return to La Estrella, as his wife yearned to do.

One morning a foreman arrived at Ibo and Lila's hut to ask them to bring a good pot of "fresh-brewed" coffee to the work camp twice a day, at dawn and early evening, and they'd be paid very well.

How wonderful! Now they would save more. With what they'd save and the possible sale of the land, they could give up that inhospitable place forever.

The wife went to the camp twice a day to bring the freshly filtered coffee.

On Saturdays many workers left to visit their families; the rest, the rowdiest ones brought women to the camp from the capital and danced to phonograph music and drank until dawn.

On those rollicking nights, Lila began to arrive home later than usual.

"Look, Lila," her husband told her one night, "I don't like this. What're you doing staying after you deliver the coffee and get the money?"

Meekly, she replied: "I stay a little while listening to the music and watching the dancing. I'm young and I like happy people . . . Why don't you come with me?"

"No, I don't like dances. I'm a shy campesino . . . OK, go on and stay a little while on Saturdays to watch the dancing but—come back early."

"Ah!"

That *ah!* revealed various movements in her soul: tenderness, gratitude, sorrow, astonishment—terror!

During the day, the carbonero worked to the noise of dredges, tractors, cement mixers, and trucks; on Saturdays, after sundown, he heard endless fragments of the music he disliked.

So it went, until that ill-fated Saturday night.

"See you, Ibo. I'm going to take them the coffee. How do you feel?"

"I've got a little fever and a headache, but it's nothing—I'm going to go to bed. The weather's horrible."

"Ah!"

She left the house and the carbonero lay down. He could hear the monotonous sounds of percussion instruments.

He managed to fall asleep about seven that night. Four hours later he awoke to the howling of rainy gusts of wind, so cold they covered everything with frost. His wife still hadn't returned.

What could've happened to her? . . . Did she freeze on the path? . . . Did a tree fall on top of her? . . . Did the wind smash her against the rocks? . . .

He got up, shielding himself as best he could. He grabbed his cape, his knife, and his lantern and took the shortcut, searching in the ditches and the undergrowth.

He arrived at the camp; the door was unbolted. Pushing the door slowly, he went in. It was a rather large shelter, furnished with about twenty cots, a number of chairs, and two huge tables at the far end of the barracks. There was no light at the entryway, but on the tables and hanging from the framing a few oil lamps burned.

At the tables several men and women were drinking liquor,

singing, and laughing riotously. The shelter was full of smoke, the smell of alcohol, and hot musical rhythms. Some of the couples were dancing lasciviously.

The carbonero stayed next to the door, in the dimness, contemplating the revelry. No one noticed his presence.

Suddenly, he spotted his wife. With a glass in her hand, she was laughing flirtatiously, sitting on the lap of a young strapping, blond tractor-driver.

The tractor-driver was the first to notice the carbonero's presence. He moved the girl off him, got up slowly, walked toward Ibo, and said:

"Hey, carbonero! . . . You want a drink?"

"No! . . . I want my wife!"

"Then take her. She's yours."

Lila emptied her glass in one gulp, wiped her mouth with the back of her hand, and staggered toward her husband. With her hands on her hips, she stood in front of him at disdainful attention.

"So—you came to spy on me? . . . Go spy on your pack of mules, I'm not one of them! I got tired of being shut up in that horrible hut. I'm young and I've got a right to amuse myself now and then. Go on, get out of here, I'll come in a bit." And in a still more aggravated tone, she added: "Carbonero!"

Ibo said nothing. With a slight sad smile he turned half-around and left.

A cold disconcerted mood hung over the camp, colder than the summit of Cerro de la Muerte.

Carbonero! . . . Carbonero! . . . Carbonero! . . .

Lila's voice resounded like a repeating echo in the deepest part of his soul. He had never thought it possible his wife would call him that—Carbonero!—insultingly, mockingly, instead of saying Ibo, as she'd always addressed him before, because that was his name.

His work took on a new cast. Now *carbonero* was a painful, cutting word. And to think that throughout his life it had been a sign of industry, decent and clean, despite the black of the charcoal!

He had just lost faith in his wife and, from then on, he would look at her with distrust; even more so because she should have come back immediately to be with him when he was sick.

Perhaps he would have forgiven her, because he understood her happy, youthful nature and her reasons for occasionally going to a party. Perhaps he would have thought about Lila's torture, about a cold black prison in the middle of a hostile mountain . . . Perhaps, also, he would have forgiven her for having sat on the lap of that man—if she had just not called him carbonero, humiliating him. So much for her, now that she'd been found carousing with bums and prostitutes.

He also felt that it was an affront to all the carboneros in the world; and to his dead mother, whose son was a carbonero, and to all the mothers of all the carboneros.

Blinded by grief, he took things to heart painfully; the handful of charcoal that wounded him was burning.

Now, in his hut, he repeated loudly what he had said on the road coming home from the camp.

"I must punish her! I must get revenge! I have to find something to humiliate her while she's alive!

"Ah! . . . as she says."

From the camp an Afro-Cuban rhythm was heard intermittently, its high notes frozen on the path so only the deep ones arrived, along with the drumbeats that seemed to say: *Car-bo-nero! Car-bo-nero!*

The wind came through the cracks like thin sheets and through the holes like filaments of ice.

Shivering through his fever, he looked out the door of the hut, contemplating the oak grove. To him it had always seemed full of a wild beauty, but now he saw it as fickle, monstrous, terrifying.

He closed the door and went to poke the hearth. Seeing the embers, he thought about his wife's pretty face, her pale, clear skin that he had observed so many times illuminated by the fire.

With an effort he shook off his gloomy thoughts and began thinking about the firewood he had to cut the next day. He took his knife and started sharpening it on the whetstone in the kitchen. But his thoughts returned to his wife, because she, Lila, his torturer, had given him that knife.

With a new effort he turned his mind to his patient, faithful mules, and he remembered that he needed new cords for hitching them.

There, on the wall, hanging from a hook, were several meters of maguey rope about as thick as a finger.

He took down the roll, took his sharpened knife, and cut a pretty long piece.

The sight of the cord in his hands made him go back to thinking about a punishment for his wife. That cord was a whip, a scourge that would leave eternal tracks on a face that would no longer be radiant.

Sometimes punishments are more monstrous than their crimes.

His mood now began to change; he was once again feeling meek, defenseless, subdued, like a caged beast.

Calmed, he walked through the room. He came upon a

picture of the Lord of Good Hope that was tipped over, and he set it back up. He opened the door, took several steps outside, and came to a nearby tree trunk where some orchids in bloom looked like tiny red hearts. He pulled a bunch of them out and went back in the house. He found an earthen pot, filled it with water, arranged the handful of orchids in it, and put it in front of the picture of the Lord of Good Hope. He lifted his gaze and for a long time thought . . . about nothing!

The storm had subsided and only a mournful light wind remained.

When Lila came back to the hut, in the early hours of dawn, she discovered the carbonero, calm and in the center of the room . . . hanging from a rope. To heighten his revenge and punishment, he had written on the wall with charcoal:

I forgive you.

"Ah! . . . Aaah!"

Translated by James Hoggard

The Diary

Fabián Dobles

WE UNTIE THE STRING around the loose yellow sheets the old black woman has lent us. The tiny nervous handwriting has a certain dynamic feel to it. It's written in an English that's not the least bit literary. "Diary of H. R. Sandiford and E. L. Forrester," we translate. We begin reading.

"August 10, 1911. It is raining and thundering when the ship docks in Puerto Limón. Sandiford and I smoke identical pipes. The sea, choppy. We see Negroes and whites on the dock and the banana train arriving. We disembark. Sandiford seems surprised by everything he sees. Everything is tropical and unfamiliar to me, too. We've been given good positions with the Company at the recommendation of my uncle. After all, a senator is a senator. Though he doesn't know why, Sandiford tells me that he's reminded of his home in Louisiana with its spacious porch and tall white columns. Perhaps the sight of so many Negroes reminds him of his childhood. Led by Mr. Bullitt, who has received us most graciously, we proceed to our hotel and settle into our rooms. Sandiford sleeps badly that night. He has discovered the *jejenes*. To be completely truthful, I cannot remember if I slept well or not. I drank enough. I think I dreamt abundantly. Sandiford seemed nervous when he woke up. He shook me and said he had a premonition that the tropics would swallow us up. Why the devil does he insist on including me in his premonitions?" Thus begins the diary of E. L. Forrester.

In a handwriting so similar as to make it impossible to distinguish the two, and under a heading that bears the same date, Sandiford adds by way of continuation: "We have arrived. Forrester seems interested in everything he sees. The lethargy that overpowered him during the crossing has disappeared. He gives the impression that he has donned a suit of armor and has shielded himself for the attack. I cannot help smiling at the sight of him. For my part, I have little to say. I've read so much about these lands that I feel a bit defrauded. I had expected more than this. The only thing that lives up to my expectations is the blasted heat. Forrester tells me he feels optimistic and has great hopes for certain projects, provided he can make use of funds he has deposited in the National City Bank—an inheritance from his father. No doubt, pirate blood runs through his veins. He invited me out for drinks, which did not go down well. They have left me feeling melancholic."

We continued reading, skipping paragraphs here and there since there were lots of repetition and inconsequential material. A paragraph written by one is unfailingly followed by one written by the other, all signed with an *F* or an *S*. The two men are probably close friends. Reading along, we saw some affinities between them, though they seem to be quite opposite in character. For example:

"January 21, 1913. Last night Mrs. Clark invited us to a party. I enjoyed it thoroughly. Her daughter, a darling sixteen-year-old girl, is absolutely charming. She reminded me of my cousin Georgette, though she was livelier and, I must admit, rather more plump. She is a splendid swimmer. Sandiford walked with us. His eyes were following her. It's a shame that Sandiford is so timid. He seemed ridiculous, sending languid looks in her direction. With a little more self-assurance, he would cut quite a dashing figure. If I'm not mistaken, Lucy Clark took notice of him also. F."

On the other hand, Sandiford writes: "The party at the Clarks was tedious. Miss Clark was a complete nuisance. I could not for the life of me understand how Forrester would choose to spend the afternoon courting her. The only thing I enjoyed was the fishing, though the rain—this infernal tropical rain—cut it short. Miss Clark tried several times to strike up a conversation with me, but she should know that I will have none of her Bostonian ways. I am a southerner. Forrester is a most curious fellow. He seems intent on winning the girl's affection. As for me, I wish him luck, though I see nothing good coming from it. New England chowder just does not appeal to some of us. S."

Further ahead, in 1915, one reads: "March 16. Forrester left for Cariari. He remains intent on setting up his own plantation. We discussed it, and I explained to him how the idea was foolhardy. He is more stubborn than the devil himself. He knows the difficulties only too well, yet he insists that he is a first-class businessman. It irks him to work for a salary, which is why he wants to start his own company and be his own boss. A bank in New York is to arrange a loan, to which he will add his own funds. I pity the poor bank."

Looking ahead to Forrester: "Sandiford acts like he's been struck by lightning. The tropics have left him even more dispirited and pessimistic. Try as I may, I've simply been unable to convince him to throw in his lot with my new business. Sandiford is a born loser, that's all there is to it. His damned stories of Negroes, legends, and curses have made him more withdrawn than ever. He should roll up his sleeves and plunge right into the jungle, like me." And: "October 24, 1915. Things are moving along nicely. Not as quickly as I would like, but they are moving at last. With my inheritance and the loan, I've been able to make the initial investment. I managed to convince Green, the Negro, don Barulio Canales, Smith, Rodríguez, and Lorenzo Urcuyo to cancel their delivery contracts with the Despicable Company and come over to my side. We already have good connections with an independent steamship line willing to make Limón a port of call. Sandiford still has his doubts. It's his damned prejudices that are holding him back. I really don't blame him. After all, he was raised among slaveholders and his own parents had slaves. They were southern gentry right out of Mississippi. It strikes me as odd that his years at the university were not enough to undo those idiotic ideas. You won't believe this, but he says he's afraid of the curse. Some document found in the Sandiford archives at the turn of the century has turned him into a raving lunatic."

And the other: "Today I have prayed with all my heart for Forrester. He doesn't know what he's got himself into. I prayed the way I did at home during that terrible year of the flood. Forrester thinks he has clout because of the few hundred thousand he's managed to scrape together. He doesn't realize that he is walking on quicksand. The money he's put together is just a start. This is a quagmire. He is out of his league, and his stubbornness is going to drag him under. He has turned into a complete neurotic. It's the banana fever. The union of growers he wants to organize is going to be a disaster. He should know that the Company will do whatever is necessary."

As the diary progresses, one can see how Forrester, stubborn and bold, sees himself as a knight in shining armor challenging the giant that he calls the Despicable Company. The other one, timid and fearful, is employed as an inspector general of fruit in a section of that giant and faces his inner world in a way that . . . But let's listen to Forrester:

"I'm alarmed by what happened to Sandiford. It wasn't his fault that he pulled the trigger. It's true that he takes this prejudice and nonsense about skin color seriously, but he wasn't the one who caused the tragedy. It was the Negro grower himself. The manager ordered Sandiford to reject all the fruit without explanation, and since the man was on the verge of ruin, he assaulted my nervous friend, who was only following orders. I had warned him: I told him any day now one of these barbarians is going to start making problems for you. Join our Union. But because of his obsession about not fraternizing with Negroes, I could not convince him. I'm sure he regrets it now. Myself, I could care less about the color of one's skin. If it would save my neck, I would join up with the devil himself. If Sandiford doesn't watch out, he'll end up lost. He told me about the family legend: a great-grandfather murdered a slave, whose mother, a witch doctor, put a curse on the entire family, saying that 'over the centuries the blood of the victim would pass into the murderer, and his hand would darken, his heart would darken, his soul and his face would darken.' Fools that they were, it made them even more withdrawn. Sandiford had no alternative but to kill the man, I suppose, and if not, well, perhaps it was just a small mistake. After all, he is afraid of guns. The legend made him afraid of them and of blood. Now he'll have no choice but to join us."

Sandiford writes that same day, as if none of this had happened: "I've sent a letter to my father. It seems that things

are not going well with the old man's business, and it was
my filial duty to try to cheer him up. Forrester insists that I
go over to his side, but since I've been given a promotion it
would be difficult for me to tell the general manager that I'm
leaving. Besides, I don't want to leave. Forrester and his crazy
ideas. He's all excited about his first shipment of fruit to New
Orleans. As if the Almighty Company weren't toying with
him the way a cat plays with a mouse before eating it. What's
more, he's forgetting that the Benevolent Company has
forced two-thirds of the wayward businessmen back to the
fold. At this point, he can't offer them any guarantees, and
on the other hand, the Greedy One assures them that it will
take all their fruit, albeit at rock-bottom prices. In short, the
great Forrester is nothing more than a dreamer. Poor fellow."

"November 10. Damnation, damnation, damnation. F."

"December 5. Forrester lost forty thousand dollars. The
Generous One delayed the wagons carrying his shipment of
bananas, and since the boat waits for no one, it left empty.
It's the third time this has happened. He will probably lose
his contract with the new steamship line. Forrester is a fool."

And months later: "My unfortunate friend Sandiford has
at last come and begged me to take him on as a partner. I
asked him not to insist. I don't want to confound matters by
injecting his lack of business sense into affairs that are already
complicated enough. I would rather face my responsibilities
alone. Sandiford has become sentimental. It must be the
Mediterranean blood on his mother's side. Luckily, I was
able to dissuade him. His health is declining and he seems
confused. Imagine coming out with such an idiotic remark!
He says his right hand is turning darker. Has he gone mad?
Poor Sandiford."

And the latter writes two months later: "Forrester is amazing. After all his setbacks, he has managed to convince ten more growers to stay with him. I admire him. In the final analysis, what he lacks in brains he makes up for in energy and daring. I have admonished him for his excessive drinking of late. He laughs and tells me that in the tropics alcohol is like milk."

And the other: "Sandiford deserves a monument facing the Capitol. He has lent me—against my will, I swear it—another fifteen thousand dollars. I am hopeful that my agents in London will be able to convince Lines & Lines that the fruit can weather the voyage to England and that it will find a market there. Otherwise, my application with the government is moving full speed ahead. My lawyer assures me he can obtain official guarantees that the shipments will arrive at the docks on time and without fail. I feel wonderful."

A year later Sandiford writes: "Indignant. Forrester lost his case. The Great Shrewd One has been declared free of all responsibility, though Forrester could bring suit against those unfortunate individuals who, in total innocence, derailed the wagons and dumped the bananas into the river. Nothing is to be gained from another trial, from sending five poor wretches to prison. Live and learn. My worst fears are coming true. Still I wanted to believe in the beauty of the growers' venture. But the methods employed by Old Fearful are diabolical. Forrester continues to seek solace in drink. His tolerance is admirable. He's been fighting and drinking for years, and he still knows how to laugh. He is an idiot . . . And I am a murderer!"

And Forrester: "Sandiford is a genius. His idea of dehydrating fruit to send it to distant markets is stupendous. We can reduce shipping costs and we won't be competing with the Greedy One, at least not directly. It's sort of a thick candy that we will send in boxes. We have begun to install the dehydrator, which fortunately was not too expensive. Inventors are worth their weight in gold. It's a shame that Sandiford persists in his stupid beliefs. Now he says that what started in his right hand, the hand that pulled the trigger, is spreading throughout his entire body. He's frightened, horrified at what his relatives in Baton Rouge will say when they see him with blond hair and black skin. He must be pulling my leg, but I'm not falling for it. He can't be serious. In every other respect, he seems completely sane. Take, for example, this amazing new project. We're dehydrating as fast as we can, and the results couldn't be more promising. On another topic: Mary Anne. The Negro girls here in the tropics are most entertaining."

Along the same lines—in the midst of banana trees, dreams, dehydrators, and idle days—the plot thickens. At this point we no longer skip pages. We're not searching for just the most interesting passages, but looking for certain threads pulling the story together, even though it may at times seem boring. For example:

"October 22, 1917. A poet from back home, who smoked a pipe just like us and was very boring to be sure, wrote: 'Love has surprising wings and flies from window to window in search of the butterfly of happiness.' I mention this because of Mary Anne. Mary Anne is the daughter of one of the *macheteros,* but to me she is a doe in heat. 'Love,' said the poet, 'sings its flattering truth from moon to moon and is blind.'" Four pages are filled with this infernal verse. The curious thing is that there is no F or S at the end of these pages. The order of the entries is broken. Usually F marks the initial entry and S follows directly afterward. Forrester continues writing on the same date in October:

"I sense something disturbing about Sandiford's behavior. He is falling in love with Mary Anne, too. My own relationship with her cannot exactly be called love. It's the result of the climate and the lack of . . . in any event, the girl has a refreshing natural vivacity about her and . . . yes, there is also her soul. But this business with Sandiford strikes a deeper chord. Poor devil. He is continually hopeless about his blackness, which at this point, according to him, has already seeped into his heart. Our famous dehydrated bananas are now preserves, since they never managed to dry out completely. I think we are the dehydrated ones."

In turn, the one from Louisiana adds: "It hurts me to see Forrester in his present state. The newly formed union of growers, pawns in his hand, has been reduced to dust. He continues to fight with no other ally but me. My idea was a good one, but the All Powerful has managed to have our first big shipment strategically placed next to a load of rotting hides. It arrived in London a marmalade of worms. As a practical joke it wasn't bad, but no one is left who will buy from us, as funny as it sounds. Forrester is an idiot, without a doubt, and I am too. Furthermore, he's a seasoned lush. Mary Anne, O God, Mary Anne . . . "

By January 1918, Forrester notes: "A lovely war. In Europe, for no reason at all, men are dying by the truckload in the trenches, and here we stupid banana growers are dying a slow death. Mr. Grimm has even gone so far as to tell me that he might give me a little job on some plantation or other that could make use of my considerable experience. Me, Ernest Lawrence Forrester, take 'a little job'? Damnation, damnation. If it were not for Mary Anne, I would send the whole lot of them to hell. At present I'm working like a dog to satisfy my creditors in New York. Meek as a lamb, I'm again selling my fruit to . . . I hate even to say its name . . . Sandiford, on the other hand, seems content in his own way. He's found a new way to deal with his obsession. He claims that even his hair has become black and kinky, and now he spends time with Jamaicans, whom he loathed before, with their strange rituals and ceremonies. It took him a considerable amount of time to break down the barrier—months and months of patient work before they would accept him as a comrade—and I'm afraid he's succeeded. It's the tropics, the tropics and his Mediterranean temperament. At times I think I'm the one who's got it all wrong. As far as I can tell, he's the same Sandiford I have always known. Well, he has lost his accent and he's very tan, for sure, but only because of the sun."

On the last page one reads: "July 1919. We are going to have a child. Forrester says it is his. The matter will be cleared up soon, when the baby is born. If it is completely black, it is mine. Sandiford."

"December 5, 1919. A beautiful little mulatto boy was born. Mary Anne wants to call him Lawrence, my maternal grandfather's name. I hope it won't disturb the old man's soul. The only unfortunate thing, unfortunate indeed, is that my good friend Sandiford has left in despair without saying goodbye. I have no idea what will happen to him when he arrives in New Orleans. I wouldn't be surprised if he winds up in a madhouse. Back there he won't be able to swim in both waters, black and white. It's possible that before long I'll give in and leave as well. The only problem is Mary Anne, dear sweet Mary Anne, and now, the baby. How they complicate things! There is nothing left to do but sit and smoke, drink, and watch the endless rain. Everything has gone to hell. All that's left is my pipe and Sandiford's, which he left behind."

After a time a man sent by the little old black woman came for the manuscripts. He asked us what we thought of them, and we told him that they made a lively, intriguing story.

"What ever became of Sandiford and Forrester?" we asked. And he answered:

"I don't know what happened to Sandiford. Forrester died a short time later on a binge at Cariari Banana Farm."

"How do you know all this?"

"I am Lawrence."

"Forrester . . . or Sandiford?"

The mulatto proudly shrugged his shoulders.

"I have only my mother's last name," he said, and he took the papers back to her, the little old woman.

Translated by John Incledon

In the Shadow of the Banana Tree

Carlos Luis Fallas

HERMINIO WAS A STRONG HAPPY GUY with thick
black hair and a thin ragged mustache. This was his weapon,
he used to say, for love. And it was for love, as we called it
then, that we went to Limón with a few pesos, after months
of work and abstinence, to have a roll with the whores.

We met in Andrómeda, a sad, lonely place at the end of
the line for La Estrella railways. I had broken sweat at all
kinds of work, and so had he. And we were both happy in the
river, diving after fish—*bobos* and *machacas*—when we were
able to steal some dynamite to try our luck in the pools and
eddies . . . No hole was too deep for us, no current too strong.
Perhaps that's why we were such good friends.

There was plenty of work in Andrómeda. The Company
needed to open a great swath through the mountains, breaking rocks on the banks of the river, filling and leveling and
building bridges to carry a train through the marshy virgin

Excerpted from Fallas's novel *Mamita Yunai*, published in 1941. Mamita
Yunai was the local name for the United Fruit Company. Fallas dedicated
the novel to his co-workers, the *linieros* of the Atlantic Zone.

forest, good for the cultivation of bananas, and in the process revive some of the plantations abandoned years before, when the river had carried away the old railroad. The work was pressing, and Bertolazzi, the Italian, an engineer in the service of the Company, was running his mule back and forth, keeping an eye on the workers, giving instructions to the contractors, making his measurements and insulting everyone he passed, black and white, in English, Italian, and Spanish.

We were working with Pancho, a Nicaraguan foreman with gold caps on his teeth, tall and pale and still pretty young. He was one of those who knew how to pick his men, all of them hard workers, and he was the only contractor who knew how to get them to work without complaints or protests. We got more and better food from him than from the others, a peso and a half more a day, good treatment, and he never had any problem with helping out one of his peons with a little money. And even with all that he put more cash in his pockets and finished the work first and best. He was an exceptional contractor!

Usually at three thirty in the morning, raining or not, Pancho's voice would ring out loud and clear calling his crew: "Eeeeverybodyyyy uuuup, *muchachos!* It's getting late and the table is set!"

We'd get up still yawning, give ourselves a quick wash from the big gourd, and still rubbing our eyes, straggle over to the foreman's place. He'd be walking down the hall, worrying, in his great boots that came up to his knees and his Stetson, which he wore pushed back on his head.

"What's the matter with these people?" he'd be muttering. And a few minutes later he'd head off for the dark camps.

We'd go into the meal-hall, lit by neon light and sit on the bench at a long table, where the platters of boiled bananas were already steaming. From the kitchen we could hear the sweet, timid voice of the *patrona*, his wife: "Goo' mornin' *muchachos*."

"Good morning, *patrona*!"

She spoke slowly, with the peculiar way of clipping words that Nicaraguans have, though it wasn't noticeable in Pancho's speech, even though they were both from the same place. She was very light-skinned, and short, with bright Indian-shaped eyes and smooth skin that was beginning to get splotchy from the inclement climate. You could see right away she was used to another kind of life. She had come from around Segovia and had run away from her rich land-owning family to follow the man she loved. And she was working like a mule there, cooking for his twenty workers. The jenny, which is what we called the breakfast, had to be ready for everyone at four in the morning; lunch at twelve, and supper at six . . . and that left her time to take care of the little one and make the preserves and jellies we bought from her. One day the poor thing was a little late with lunch. Pancho didn't say anything. Well-fed and heading back to our place, we could hear her shouts from the house. We took off back there as fast as we could, and after he'd kicked her to the ground, it was quite a job to get the machete he was trying to hit her with away from him.

Little by little everyone was arriving: old Jerez with his colored neckerchief tied around his throat to protect him from the cold . . . and to keep his red nose dry with the ends of it; Andrés the Cat; el Cholo; Alfonsito, the younger brother of old Jerez who no one liked because he was an annoying little pest. The "twins" arrived together like they always did: the short little pot-bellied one right on the heels of the other who looked like a ladder, he was so tall and skinny. We had baptized them the "twins" because they were so different, and because they were inseparable.

From the doorway Pancho hurried his people on. Poor Pastora ran around passing out the plates. Between jokes and smiles, the famous jenny was disappearing fast: a plate of oats, which was the "extra" Pancho usually had, a pile of rice and beans that were scrambled and fried that we called *gallo pinto*, and the steamed bananas. Then a mug of black coffee with no sugar, and we'd hit the road!

When we were leaving for work with our tools on our shoulders, only a few lights in the other camps were beginning to move around.

"Pick it up, boys, we've got a ways to go!" Pancho would say, putting himself at the front of the line and heading down the railbed.

Well into the mountain, splashing through the mud on the bed, slipping on the twisting roots, jumping over the big trunks of the recently felled trees, we could hear the sharp cock-a-doodle-doo of the roosters, far off in the distance . . .

We were almost always way up on the mountain when Herminio's cousin caught up to us; he was too fond of sleeping and too lazy to get out of bed, but he was a really good worker. One of those mornings, when it was still dark, we heard a mule trotting up behind us and without turning around, I said, "Here comes Calero the crazy man still choking down his jenny!"

And Herminio, who had a shovel on his shoulder and was holding down the end of it with his jaw and tightening the knot on his shirt, muttered, "Oh, what a cousin . . . The same old story every morning: as hard as you push him he only lets out a snore and turns over."

A minute later he was with us, snorting loudly, kicking the

mud with his great shoes, rolling his big wide-open eyes and rowdy as ever. These were the pantomimes that he usually made along the way.

"Son of a bitch!" he shouted at us. "You are all fuckers! Do you know who I was dreaming about when you woke me up! About Mister Clinton's black woman. And she'd just decided to take off her clothes . . . when you all show up and wake me up! You rats!"

Choking back laughter, I told him, "Payday is coming up, so you can quit your masturbating!"

"Payday!" he shouted, glaring at me and making an indecent gesture. "Look! Two paydays have gone by and no whores have shown up here, and I'm not going to Limón to waste the shitty money I make . . . "

Though his language was filthy—like everyone who has to study in the crude schools of the banana camps—Calero was as ingenuous as a child and had a heart of gold, open to everyone.

The three of us would go on talking together as we passed the worksites of the other peon gangs, which started work at six, and we came to a branch of the river that we had to cross, where the water was up to our chests.

"That's the only way you'll wash your belly-button, you old pig," Calero yelled to the big-bellied twin.

That twin always had his t-shirt rolled up, showing his hairy belly with its great belly-button, wrinkled and filthy.

We were all walking like ducks, with a peculiar wobble because of the heavy shoes, crude and badly made, with soles nailed up with steel taps, good for sliding with. They always made me feel like my feet were encased in concrete blocks.

Goosh . . . goosh . . . goosh went the feet with each step of the enormous shoes, filled to the top with water and mud. It was still dark, the mountain just barely awake, and we were already sweating at our work. Pancho was making his measurements, throwing the reeds he used as cords between the stakes set out by the engineer and shouting, "Now we'll see what my people are made of! This is our work for today. I'm going to help you, to see if we can get out of here before noon!"

We divided up the work in pairs: Jerez and his little brother; Calero and Andrés the Cat; the twins; Herminio and me . . .

If we were doing fill, Calero looked for the deepest and farthest parts to toss the earth from, as though to show off the strength of his arm and his skill at digging.

"I'm going to show all these little pricks—they wouldn't beat me even greased," he said, spitting loudly into his hands and throwing out challenging glances at everyone.

Whether the ground was clay or loose dirt, he dug it out in enormous shovelfuls and tossed it high . . . and each shovelful arced through the air, turning over itself without so much as a clod falling away. You could still see the shape of the shovel when the dirt thudded onto the fill. There was no way out but to try to imitate him.

Boom . . . boom . . . boom! The shovels of dirt were falling continuously, shaking the railbed, and we were all sweating, soaking the ends of the shovels.

"Come on up, boys!" shouted the foreman. "It's OK here, now we have to even it up."

We climbed up, bent over from the pain in our backs, leveled it up, and returned to the hole. In a little while we were all stripped to the waist, and the sweat was running in rivers and blinding our eyes, drenching our pants, sliding down our arms . . . And on like that for hours and hours until we felt nauseous, and our legs were shaking, and there was a terrible hammering in our heads.

Heavy, suffocating heat was slowly gripping the whole mountain. Not a leaf was moving; not a breeze blew. Everything was stupidly immobile, as though all of nature had been turned into lead . . . We went on sweating over the shovels . . . boom . . . boom . . . boom!

The sun was shining in the cloudless sky, pouring fire onto our naked backs, scorching everything, making us see red blobs in the air and hear incredible choruses of crickets buzzing in our heads.

Only the weather-beaten shoulders of the banana workers didn't get blistered from the sun.

Water! Waaaaterrr!

Pancho sent the younger Jerez brother to bring water for everyone. And the bucket came around with water from the swamp, as warm and thick as linseed oil, cloudy from the mud and the residue from the rotting trees. One by one we glued ourselves to the bucket's lip. Calero always waited until last so he could stick his head right into it and drink with great gulps, imitating the mules.

"You'll fill your gut with amoebas and hookworms!" I told him once.

"What can I drink then? This is linseed oil. Other times it's like an eggnog, but with little frog's eggs instead."

The sky would suddenly get dark, the clouds thunder, the wind blow loudly, shaking the mountain, the howler monkeys would roar . . . and a minute later we'd be shoveling yellow mush and shivering from the cold . . . Then the sun fell on our backs again, drying out our clothes almost instantly and forcing a hot steam to rise from the earth, asphyxiating us, and again the muggy stillness, and the suffocation of the sweat . . . then water again . . . then more sun . . . And that's how it went until noon almost every day. Sometimes we left a little earlier, when we sweated more.

Other times it was laying track, handling the heavy ties full of steel-like splinters that ripped our necks, shoulders, and hands, and swinging the mallets with our noses almost stuck to the rails. Or we demolished the mountain to open up the route, or used machetes to clean the creeks where the bridges would be built.

We'd start back like beaten dogs, padding along in complete silence. Only Calero still had enough stuff left to throw stones at the monkeys or to make jokes and tease everyone. We threw ourselves into the water to cross the river again and soon were calling out to the people working for the engineer and other contractors who didn't get off until four.

"Get to work, you camels!" Calero would shout at them.

"Shut up, you wet-butt!" was the usual reply.

Whenever we passed the first downed trees near the camps, Herminio stopped to have a look at the enormous ones that had been felled by the axes.

One day, pointing at a gigantic trunk, he said to me, "Look at that beauty! You can't even reach the edge on your tiptoes!" He was quiet for a moment and then muttered, "Why does the Company import this crappy pine for the camps? Look at all this waste. If they'd put a mill here, they'd have enough wood to pile up forever!"

"There are millions and millions of feet of oak and cedar

and laurel and all kinds of good wood rotting here as fertilizer for the bananas!" I told him. "But what does it matter to those guys if they don't pay for it. Even the climate is going to change from our messing around with the mountains . . . !"

LA PASTORA SERVED us a little soup, beans, rice, and bananas for lunch. The other gangs made do with bananas, beans, and rice—or with rice, beans, and bananas.

If by chance we had any dynamite, we'd go to the river. Calero'd go along with us to have rights to the catch, but he was useless in the water. When we blew a deep hole, he'd jump right in with a big splash . . . and start paddling around like a puppy dog, with his head and his butt sticking out; then he'd get out, snorting and waving his arms around like a windmill . . . and with his hands empty. If we sent him to the rear to watch for the *bobos* that were getting by us, he was on the bank in a second, hurling curses at the stones and rubbing his shins.

And he'd stay there, firmly seated, while Herminio and I searched the bottom again and again until we were exhausted or let ourselves be dragged by the currents after the slippery animals, knocking against the rocks and the tree trunks.

When we were lucky we had enough of a load for all three of us. Calero would separate out the iridescent green *machacas* we'd blown up, which weren't much good for anything but soup because they have so many tiny bones. But if you put them in a big cloth sack and boil them real good, they make a healthy and delicious hot broth.

"Very pretty these little suckers, but so cunning!" he would say as he threw them off to the side while grabbing his throat, pretending he already had a bone in it.

From the middle of the river we tossed *monjarras* or *viejitas* at him just to bug him. These fat little fish were a color between red and black, with even blacker rings around their bodies and armed with a sharp, bony spine on the top fin.

"Don't throw that garbage!" Calero would shout furiously, blowing on a finger and sucking the blood running from it. And these too kept company with the *machacas*.

In a separate pile he put the *bobos* with their white bellies and shiny black bodies turning opaque as the thick skin dried in the air. Some were almost a yard long, fat and round, with flat heads and hard snouts, white and rough, whose tip was raised as though it were smelling something bad. When one of them, not completely dead, beat its tail on the ground, Calero would assure it by saying: "Be quiet, you devil! What's the rush about going into the pot!" And he'd lick his lips in anticipation of the delicious white meat, almost completely free of treacherous bones.

With the *bobos* went the mid-sized, plump *tepemechines* with tiny gray scales; and the rare *guabinas*, pointed at the tail with a big head and thick whiskers on a wide nose and a white pouch stuck on their belly; and the smooth, silvery *roncadores*. And once in a while a *róbalo* with flesh so delicate we couldn't leave it even for a day in brine—that was one of the best fish to be found in the river.

We never stopped risking our lives in our river adventures. Besides the danger that the dynamite would blow up in our hands—because we used a short fuse so the fish wouldn't have time to get away—and the chancy currents and the treacherous hidden rocks, there were plenty of crocodiles in the river. One afternoon we were diving in a deep pool when Herminio suddenly surfaced all red in the face and blowing streams of water from his nose and mouth. I didn't pay any attention to him and dived into the hole. I went steadily down, releasing little bubbles of air from my nose until I got to the bottom and turned around and around with my eyes peeled, without the usual burning feeling, and I stretched out my hands to feel all over the bottom. I was running out of breath and thinking of heading for the surface when I made out the dim white shape of a *tepemechín* in the dark water. I had just put my hand on it when I saw another one a little farther on, and even though I was almost ready to explode, I tried to bring it up too. I had barely touched it when the fish stopped moving its tail and slowly descended a little farther. I swam desperately and then . . . it stopped again! One last try and I got it, already beginning to swallow water. It was time to surface, but my head hit a rock so hard that it sent reverberations into my brain. I moved to the side and bumped it again; then to the other side and there too . . . I was stuck in a cave!

My heart stopped, paralyzed with terror. I released my catch and began to swim backwards desperately, like a crab, swallowing water, seeing rings of fire everywhere, and at the point of feeling like I was dying, I got into a crouch on the bottom and sprang upward like a shot, willing to smash my head on the rocks . . .

I came out all purple, blowing water through my nose and mouth and feeling a burning pain in my temples. I collapsed like a log on the bank.

Calero, who was sitting on a rock waiting for the fish, hadn't been worried about my long dive, since I was one of those who could stay down longer than anyone. Herminio had been worried, though, and when he saw me fall down, he ran over, saying: "What happened! Did you get stuck in a crocodile cave?"

I could barely nod yes before he added, "You didn't give me time to warn you, brother . . . The same thing happened to me!"

Another time, diving near a deep dark bank, Herminio surfaced and began swimming desperately toward the shore, reaching out his hands for me to help him out. His body was shaking, his face was bright red, and once he could stop his teeth from chattering, he pointed to the spot with horror and exclaimed, "Sonnnovabitchhhh! Right there on the bottom . . . a terrible crocodile."

"A crocodile?"

"Yes! I thought it was a big *róbalo*, and I put my hand on its back. The way it turned!"

That's why, even with the terrible food, almost no one else dared to look for the fish that could be caught only with dynamite. We couldn't find any poisonous mullein in the mountains; casting nets were really expensive and nobody made them there anyway; and the fish didn't bite at hooks.

"What do *bobos* eat?" Calero asked once.

"Drool from the rocks," Herminio answered. "Haven't you ever seen where the water is clear how they pass like shadows over the rocks underwater? They swim against the current and come back again sucking . . . Until the rock is all smeared black from where they were nosing at it!"

There was always a party at camp when we emptied the sacks, and everyone was all smiles, shouting with happiness.

"Don't make such a racket!" we'd tell them. "The rest will notice, and the blacks will smell them, and then the whole world will be over here wanting us to sell them some . . . u̓ even the Italian hears the rumor. Then we'll really be in great shape!"

Only the Company could use dynamite, and it was absolutely forbidden for anyone else. Whenever Bertolazzi, the engineer, got wind that we'd gone down to the river, he began to make inquiries and he'd often threaten to send the police after us.

"That disgraceful Italian, as long as he's stuffed, he doesn't care if his peons are fed like pigs!" Calero would say furiously. "He's lucky we don't stuff them right up his snout!"

"No, my frien'. What that sly dog wantz iz for uz to spend our little money at the comp'ny store, buyin' the stinking stuff they have for sale there!"

"And they charge pure gold for it!" interrupted old Jerez, neckerchief in hand and rubbing his nose harder than ever.

So we couldn't let anyone outside our group know. We'd smuggle one over to Clinton, our black friend, though, because he always shared some of the *tepezcuintles* he killed with us.

And that was how, running risks like that, we would break up the monotonous menu. And that was already after the extra of the oats! The others had to make do with bananas, rice, and beans for lunch . . . and rice, beans, and bananas for supper!

Translated by Will Kirkland

The Oropéndolas

Quince Duncan

. . . and the voice said "no,"
and so just because of that, here it is . . .

THEY ALWAYS FLY in the protection of the gods. Mornings, they streak across the sky southward; at dusk they return, the sunset in tow behind their yellow tails.

On the water one notices: the reflection of the oropéndolas is adorned in a crystal regalia. From the depths, from the deepest spot in the river; in the sky, higher than the leafy heights of the *pejibaye* tree, and more significantly day by day, as the years passed by over our innocent heads.

Every day we went to see them, and on our daily pilgrimage we learned to love them. We never knew how to explain why it never occurred to them to move their nests closer to Mr. Fredric's cornfield. They never gave it a thought. At least that's what Ronald and I figured in those times that will always resonate in our deepest memories.

We were twelve years old. At that age, just as we had awakened from the lethargy of childhood, everything became motivated by passions. Our devotion to the oropéndolas brought us the implacable punishment of our elders who didn't understand the great truth: we weren't escaping the house to do wrong, like they said, but rather to be poets.

Daily, in the shade of trees, quiet as life itself and like life itself, palpitating with restlessness, we shed the contradictions of our beings in the intense love that we are all capable of at twelve years old.

We never dared disturb the peace of our friends. We watched them from afar, feeling a part of their games and disputes. Fascinated, we dreaded the forest noises, afraid they would rob us of such priceless companionship.

Time passed quietly over our hands and faces, revealing to us moment by moment the intimacies of nature.

One day, however, we got the idea to invite another friend to our daily rendezvous. Neither Ronald nor I has forgiven ourselves for this serious mistake, because the truth is, we could have imagined that our friend would bring along a bow and arrow.

Like always, at sundown the oropéndolas flew in the protection of the gods. They streaked across the sky northward, their yellow tails shimmering, and in tow behind them, the last breath of twilight. We watched them pass overhead with a sorrow that pierced us to the depths of our spirit. To the place of our daily rendezvous, there to Mr. Fredric's cornfields, they would never return.

Maybe they couldn't forget that there, one sunny morning over the glistening greenness of the fields, the earth caressed the rigid body of a friend killed by treachery.

Translated by Zoe Anglesey

From

Deeper Than Skin

Abel Pacheco

DISCOVERY

Being kids with Felipe!

As far as I'm concerned, there's never been anyone as great as him.

Who else could shinny up a coconut tree with so much grace?

Back then it pained me to be such a paleface around so many chocolate-colored kids.

I was part of a minority, but things were easy, because no one knew it.

There were more important things than the color of your skin: having more *chumicos*, jumping higher, being brave enough to dive into the river from the highest rock.

One day some outsiders came, and I heard them talking with Papa about "the blacks."

My old man contradicted the strangers, who'd said they were loafers, inferior types.

I sensed Dad was defending me because I was part of the barefoot, loud-mouthed crew that had stolen Mr. Jones's *yocotó* leaves.

But when my friends came for me the next day, things weren't the same. Felipe noticed that someone had sown a bad seed in me, the seed of our difference.

In the swimming hole he put his black hand on my arm and kept looking at me.

"White," he told me, angry at having been deceived.

I felt ashamed.

I didn't say good-bye to him when the train snatched me away from the banana plantation and the rails of my childhood.

PAPA URIAH

Papa Uriah came when the world was new, even before we had the line.

There were only howler monkeys and parrots and this Pacuare River that had been around forever.

It was so long ago that Christ hadn't come, and God was black like us and you had to dance for him, not pray to him.

Besides things being happier then, you didn't have to give him money; he was satisfied with the white rooster we offered him from time to time.

He even visited us while we cut through the forest and sowed the earth with a long line of railroad ties and corpses.

Papa Uriah did not get sick because he spoke with Changó in his own tongue.

It's not true that he kidnapped the little gringo girl. What happened was, she went into the jungle and played and played with the spirits in the rivers until she was changed into a golden orchid.

But we blacks died, and kept on dying, from that vomiting in the barracks.

Papa called the gods and they stopped the plague.

But being so good, they couldn't ask for the life of a little girl in exchange. Just a rooster, a white rooster . . .

That's why what the whites did was bad.

Of course he was only a black man, but smearing him with honey and tying him down on a *zompopa* ant hill is bad even for them, who of course are going to Heaven.

A VERY VERY OLD MAN TOLD ME

No, life isn't a game in these parts.

You make an enemy and suddenly a toad may be growing in your belly, or an iguana.

Things of the Pocomía, man . . .

That must be the thing.

It's like a curse, but here, the highway's never going to get this far.

They say it's very difficult because of all the rocks, the cold, the mountains so dense that not even an agouti can get through.

But what I don't understand is why—when Mistuh Guardia, when Mistuh Keith—they could do it.

Things of the Pocomía, man . . .

In those days there was no machinery besides the muscle and drive of the Caribbean people.

Yeah, of the Caribbean people, back when there wasn't any Coca-cola.

And see, it's already going on a hundred years since we made a path, but one of iron, not like the kind they make now with those flimsy materials like honeycomb.

The old path is still here, but the new one . . . at the first storm it changes into a mushy *guanábana* passage.

I haven't understood yet why my late wife Charlotte said that in these days men need only two things.

Things of the Pocomía, man . . .

MAYBE SO

If she was or wasn't, it's hard to know now.

The fact is that since she was a little girl I know how upset she got when the full moon rolled up on the mountains, filling the Pacuare with colors and shadows.

One fine day she blossomed into adolescence, like something popping out overnight.

Good at washing, and everything else.

The only problem was when the moon got all fat-faced and looked like it was beckoning to her.

No one, nothing could stop her.

A thousand fireflies would shine in her eyes and she would seem to have lost her mind, while at the same time she would purr.

Naked, she would charge into the forest, and when she'd return she'd be panting and shivering.

When they followed her, men lost track of her in the jute growing on the riverbank.

One day, with a paca-hunting dog, they managed to cross the barrier of jute following her trail.

Among the heliotropes, they saw her making love with a jaguar.

Of course, the dog yelped.

The couple fled to the forest, and in the moonlight it looked like the tracks had been made by two jaguars.

MULES

Now the fruit isn't carried by mules.

Now there are revolving cables full of hooks where the bunches are hung, and where in an orderly fashion, they disappear among the branches.

It's like a long, endless, blind snake.

It's not like the mules—you had to speak to them and scratch them and give them salt, and even then sometimes they didn't feel like carrying the bunches or trotting between puddles to pull the *burrocar*.

What became of the mules?

Did they kill them?

Did they let them go into the mountains, knowing that they, thanks to man, couldn't even breed?

Who knows. Not one linesman, from all those out there, has been able to answer me.

Last night I dreamt that another machine had arrived, one that cut the bunches, removed the flowers, wrapped them, and hoisted them onto the boat.

In the dream, I asked: what became of the men?

SUCURÚ

Sucurú the skinny man.

Alone. Alone.

All alone.

Better that he didn't talk. When he did, he flooded the air with an odor that escaped in burbles. And in his practice of robbing tombs, he had found only some stones and the stench of a thousand Indian graves that had lodged in his lungs.

On the trail of the so-called golden tapir, he had been silently crisscrossing the jungle forever.

So much *garrobo* meat had given him beady eyes and a slithery walk.

No one ever knew a woman or a friend of his, and the old folks said that long ago he had come from far away, and that he'd always been the same: a skinny mestizo carrying the bar he used for searching tombs, and selling pots to get by, poorly fed and unkempt.

When he crossed the forest, Sucurú was just another vine,

and he slept curled up in a tree without getting hurt by a *toboba* or a jaguar.

One night two drunks stole two little pieces of jade from him and broke his pots.

He didn't say anything . . .

Curiously, the next day the two died from snakebites.

The priest, holding up his crucifix, told Sucurú to get out of town.

He didn't say anything . . .

Like a kid, his only reply was to stick his tongue out at the priest.

A long tongue, long and forked at the end.

THE GUARANTEE OF A CONTRACT

Callaghan laid sixty clean bunches of bananas next to the line. Bunches with a lot of hands; hands with a lot of fingers. Sixty bunches: twenty to pay debts, thirty-five for salt, some raw sugar, codfish, and corn.

All of them with red flowers, their skin the soft green of motmot feathers.

Five for five hopeful little black children on Christmas Eve.

The ones from the Company passed by, buying fruit.

Callaghan didn't know about saturated markets in a faraway country way up north.

Coarse as he was, he had no way of knowing about telegrams with orders not to buy.

Coarse as he was, he believed in the contract that obliged the Company to buy all the healthy fruit that he would carry to the rails.

The men told him that his proudly grown bunches were no good.

That they were infected with fungus, that the fingers were small, that they didn't have enough hands.

They took twenty so that Callaghan would be grateful, so that he'd go on driving the mule and bringing bananas.

The other forty remained there, becoming wormy the way Christmas Eve dreams of five little black children became wormy with disappointment.

THE DOGS

I . . .

Before it was me and my dogs . . .

Tilín, Roto, and Colorado used to go with me to the forest. Together we'd look for a feeding ground.

We'd lie in wait.

We'd fall on the prey.

We liked the smell of fresh deer blood and feeling the palm fronds quiver at the step of the tapir.

When we got home together, I carried the dead animal, and it was nice to feel its warmth against my neck.

The four of us bent down by the path, and I remembered the time when María and the babies were still around.

They had to go back to town when the corn wasn't paying off, and the plot was getting overgrown.

They were going to come back when the price of corn went up, if it went up.

Who knows how long ago that was. I stayed with Tilín and Colorado and Roto.

Later the jungle fell in the wake of the Company, which was surrounding our plot.

Everything was made harder for us four, but I didn't want to sell. Because of hoping that María would come back.

The gringos said rabies was a danger.

Rabies?

I buried them alongside each other under a *jaquí* tree.

I also buried my shovel and my pick there.

But not my rifle.

RAIL

It had stricken him, like grief, and he stared at the rails all day.

He didn't know why or for what—it was just to see, nothing more, interrupted only by the train going by.

The train made him furious, butting into his rail-world without permission.

That's what it was, a rail-world: smooth, hard, cold, gray, that imperturbably crossed both rock and swamp.

He hadn't spoken with anyone for a long time, much less with her.

That's the way he was, like now. It was a lie that that man with the strong laugh had ever existed.

She had made him into that amorphous, smiling creature that danced and danced.

But it had been so nice to see her shake her blonde hair and to enjoy her saying happily:

"You folk really are happy."

"You folk really have rhythm."

"You folk really feel the music."

You, you, you, you.

Then came the day when seeing her so happy he wanted to kiss her.

Better look at the rail.

The world is a rail.

Always hard, gray, cold, smooth.

CONGOLÍ

That cinnamon-colored boy with a laugh like a jay is worth a lot.

Congolí, noisy like a flock of macaws, happy, leaping little frog *cocoi*.

"Yes, sir! A smart boy, willing, alert."

"You have to help Congolí."

And they helped him . . .

He went to the capital.

Good-bye, you rivers Chirripó and Pacuare. Good-bye, *yocotó* and *coconó*.

Good-bye, *calalú* and *chiainarrú*.

A new world: shoes, high-school uniform, Sunday communion.

You don't say "ain't no good."

You don't laugh like a jay.

Congolí in algebra and in Latin. In the "poor little black boy" party, in "we are all equal, but don't look at the white girls." In "use only this washcloth." In "look at the little black boy we're educating."

Bad grades . . . bad moods.

Downcast looks and dark tears in a dark room.

Congolí fled.

On foot by the line and one mild yawning morning, a jay's laugh bounced on the stones of the Pacuare.

Lazy black, sonofabitchen black, thankless black.

JUAN CHAC

Juan Chac had for his world that hut that Sibu encircled in his goodness with *pejibayes,* red-orange like the sun when it sinks behind Monte Utyum.

Juan Chac was rich: he had an immense jungle, he had corn, he had a magnificent river from which he took silver fish with a long arrow, a long, serrated arrow.

Juan Chac had corn liquor, he had a woman, he had seven valiant Indian children.

To the Indian he was rich.

To the white he was poor: he didn't have rum or a car or neckties, and he never traveled farther than Táberi.

The whites offered him a hundred pesos to plant and watch over some chamomile shoots.

Juan wanted to buy his woman a grinder so she wouldn't have to bend over the stone, and he planted the chamomile.

The other whites arrived with a stick and some rope, with cries of "Indian bastard."

Juan Chac arrested for being bad, for being a corruptor, for planting marijuana.

TURTLES

When the crashing wave breaks, they jump onto the shore.

They turtle along, dragging their shells in a rhythmic centuries-old minuet.

They spawn deep in the sand, and when they attempt their return, they are flipped belly up and are left, flapping in vain, rocking back and forth stubbornly on their shells.

Turtle in the soup, eggs in the gut of some turtle-bashing drunk.

Sure, God made the animals first and then man.

If the animals are dying, does the diviner divine who's next?

Translated by James Hoggard

The Blue Fish

Julieta Pinto

DREAMS FLED INTO HIDING on contact with the light, and his sleepy eyes began to receive images that awakened reality in his mind. The last minutes before falling asleep and the first on awakening are states that do not permit one to feel either dead or alive, like intermediate steps from light to shadow in which the ability to see is lost and confusion reigns. Little by little, familiar shapes stand out, and the mind, distressed at leaving mysteriously attractive and unknown areas, begins to calm itself and, by means of relationships, locates itself in space. I am me, I am alive, this is my house. But that morning it was not his house. A strange room, different objects, startled him and only once he sat up did he realize that he was not dreaming, and he remembered that he had arrived at Puerto Limón two days ago. The plane trip had been quite an experience. Holding on to his mother's hand he had felt his heart accelerate along with the engine. When the noise indicated maximum speed and the plane shook on taking off from the earth with the effort of a soul departing the body, he had squeezed his mother's hand and closed his eyes in fear. A few moments later, feeling himself being rocked among the clouds, he opened his eyes and was amazed to see the roofs of the houses disappear in the distance as the blue mountains came closer. White clouds, like veils of mist, crawled through the valleys, and they were so delicate he could see through them. How free he felt when he was above the earth! He knew the height of the mountain, and to see it looking like a blue miniature, like the one his mother always put in the Nativity scene, made him feel drunk with the strength and power a man feels on conquering nature, even if only for brief moments. The trip was short, and he kept his eyes wide open so as not to miss a single detail of the constantly changing landscape unfolding before his eyes. The motionless rivers seemed to be sleeping, as if immobilized by a magic spell, and the trees grew bigger as they approached the ocean, not only because the plane was losing altitude but also because the vegetation grew taller and thicker, as if to pit its strength against the ocean's and show that it would fight if invaded. He remembered the excitement of landing, how a gray strip widened until there was enough room for the silver wings to fit, and the roar of the waves when the engine was turned off. A trip on a bus took them past tumbledown houses whose porches were filled with black youngsters of all sizes, their naked bellies sporting their navels like misplaced buttons. They waved their arms wildly, greeting the driver. Watching the bus go by was probably one of their favorite diversions and helped them forget the hunger pangs that racked their young bodies. You could see the misery in the houses that were falling apart, in the people dressed in rags, and in the haggard faces of the old folks, with dark stooped bodies.

The hotel looked like any other hotel, but the owners had added their personal touch of spontaneous charm, a charac-

teristic of everyone in the port: the driver, the owner of the
boat, the man who rented bicycles, even the little boy who
sold lottery tickets and whose wistful expression convinced
the mother to buy one. They all had an agreeable and cheerful attitude, quite unlike the sullen inhabitants of the capital.
Everyone wanted the visitors to know and love their city as
they themselves did. They suggested new places, which were
never disappointing, because the tropical beauty of the Atlantic was beyond what anyone could imagine. His eyes still held
reflections of the Mohín River, its banks drenched in green,
reflected in ripples of quiet water, and the marvelous beach
they found on disembarking. It was a narrow strip of land
that struggled to survive between the ocean and the river.
The coconut palms with their green and gold leaves were
unaware of the danger they lived in: as languorous as women
in hammocks, they swayed back and forth without worrying
about the weather. His heart beat faster at the memory of the
train whistle—which sounded at the precise moment he was
crossing the bridge to return home—and the terror he felt
when the vibrations went through his body, transmitted by
the boards that lined both sides of the bridge, offering protection in case of emergency. And an emergency it was. If it
had not been for a fisherman who was there and held on to
him with strong arms, he might have thrown himself into
the river out of desperation at seeing the oncoming train. It
seemed to him that the boards weren't strong enough to support him, his mother, and the fisherman. As the train went
by the three of them almost lost their footing. But when he
reached firm land, he felt years older and very proud of what
he would tell his playmates. His spirit absorbed the beauty
of beaches like Portete and of far corners where the tropical
vegetation exploded with new shoots and leaves, of sunsets

doubled by their reflection in the ocean, of the moon coming out when the sun was hidden, as if it felt obliged to take its place in order not to leave the sky sad and alone in the darkness. The moon's pale light was a sad copy of the sun's, but on being reflected in the ocean it acquired a misty tone that filled its surroundings with melancholy and created another ocean, mysterious in the light of its waves.

Everything interested and excited him, but from the moment he saw the blue fish, everything else dissolved into a kaleidoscope of figures and landscapes that served as a backdrop for this ideal creature. The fish ruled as lord and master of his thoughts, with the force of first love and the same persistence, so that even after it is finally over, it tries to return in the melody of a song or the color of a flower. He had seen it the day before, when they went to the island of La Uvita. The boat, at the speed of a darting fish, sprayed drops of salty water over his face, rosy with happiness and sunshine. The island was only a short distance away, and the calmness of the ocean made the trip even shorter. The ocean was a copy of the sky in a slightly darker tone, and the crests of foam were like brushstrokes breaking the monotony of the color. The uninhabited island was a refuge of trees and plants, a dark green stain competing with the brilliant blue that surrounded it, and its coral reefs protected it from the fury of the waves on stormy nights . . . On calm days when the tide was rising, the water would furiously push its way out, bursting in sprays of foam on reaching a hole in the coral. Soaring several meters, it would then fall exhausted by the effort. The water was absorbed immediately, and silence prevailed for a few minutes, to be interrupted by the special sound, like fleeing crabs, of a new spray of foam. The nests of wild ducks balanced on the highest rocks, and the parents flapped their wings, protecting their young from the danger of intruders. They would leave for a while, their agile bodies dropping to the ocean as if shot by an arrow: seconds later they would come up triumphantly, with a little fish in their partly open beaks.

The marine life on the rocks was strange and looked amazingly like flowers and fruits. On the other hand, the algae and coral at the bottom of the rocks, seen through the transparent water that moved with the waves, looked like sea creatures. Leaning over to contemplate all the beauty, he saw a flash of blue lightning that disappeared in an instant, to reappear again. At first he didn't believe it was a fish. The blue was the same as the color of the butterflies that flitted across the pastures of the *Meseta Central*. The sunlight reflected on it so brilliantly as it moved through the water that it looked like an engraving on blue foil. The fish seemed to know this and displayed its beauty with gentle motions. Sometimes a wave would carry it away, and just when the boy was losing hope of seeing it again, it would reappear with a flash of blue. The island's enchantment vanished, the sea urchins and conches no longer interested him; he was held in thrall observing the fish intently and longing to hold it in his hands to see if it was real. His knees hurt from kneeling, and his hand tried unsuccessfully to catch it. Though annoyed, he obeyed the third time his mother called him to hurry because the boat was about to leave. He fell asleep dreaming of holding it in his hands and discovering the secret of its brilliance. The memory seared his mind again, and he got up hurriedly to go to the island. This time he really would catch it. He took a little butterfly net with him, sure that he would capture it. When he asked the boat owner about the blue fish, the owner looked at him curiously and said he had never heard anything about fishes that color. But he was so sure of his fish, he wanted to show it to everyone so they wouldn't think the sun had caused him to imagine it. As soon as they arrived at the island, he went back to the same place where he had seen it the day before. It didn't take long for the fish to appear, and the boy was excited at seeing it. The fish seemed even more brilliant than the day before, and he became so absorbed in watching it that he forgot the net. The fish moved faster and faster; it seemed to multiply until there were three or four fishes in its place. Then it would tire and rest, and in the stillness it looked like a butterfly on a stone flower. During one of these rests, he lowered the net cautiously, caught the fish in it, and pulled it out, enjoying in anticipation the result of his catch. It was a great surprise to see the net empty. Thinking that the fish had slipped out at the last minute, he tried again—with the identical result. He tried impatiently to catch it again and again, but when he was sure it was in his power, there was only water running through the holes in the net. And the fish, unafraid of the danger, returned again and again, moving rapidly or keeping as still as an inanimate object.

His tired arm and numb knees were proof of the long hours he had spent in the same position dipping the net. He heard his mother's voice. She was anxious because the boat would not wait, and they had to return to the capital that day. He threw away his useless net, left the island, and departed from the port.

Years later, whenever happiness that had been within arm's reach vanished for no logical reason, he always remembered the blue fish transformed into bubbles of foam.

Translated by Angela McEwan

The Spirit of My Land
Yolanda Oreamuno

I AM FILLED with my own thoughts. Filled inside like a clay jug filled with water. I have thought about the wind. I must think about its thread traversing the earth to find what I'm looking for. But today, I don't know when, at what instant, I thought about the spirit of my land. I sensed it; but I don't know where. I know I have to follow the thread of the wind to find it, the wind that travels from north to south, knows the seas, strolls down streets, and gets tangled up in the forest. To find what I'm looking for, and what I sense and divine without realizing, I have to follow the thread of the wind.

Starting where it gets bored playing alone on the savanna. Where the earth is parched and burning, where the sun isn't content with fondly caressing the shape of things, where it gets into the pith of trees and the marrow of men. There, where it has stripped vast horizons bare of silhouettes. There in the north. The land has been stretched like a quilt over a bed and, stretched and open, it's still looking for its skeleton. Mornings dawn like one great rosy opening after another, the air vibrates endlessly, and the echo seems to laze around in the elements. Everything is full, hot, dense, the land stretched, no little patches of shade, no little nests of even slight cool, the land strewn upon itself, deceitful, horizontal. In the summer, weather-beaten and grimy like street kids on whom filth has molded a likeness of themselves. The true land seems to be under that cloak—in the summer, dust, and in the winter, mud, which is the earth lying down on itself. The marrow, the heart of all that, is many feet below what we see outlined shining at the horizon and far beyond the horizon. In the winter, the land, the true land—the one that feeds the cattle grazing on its vast spaces and remains steadfast—it becomes nothing more than a semblance of itself, changed into a splashing and slippery lagoon, softened sucking mud under the hooves of a horse, its loins layered with sweat, its muzzle flared and panting. The horse looks for support from the true land, the one that he recognizes, that gives him pasture and shelter, that doesn't deceive him like that other land. The true land below the one masquerading, pretending to be the horizon; the true land that the tree roots and the horse's hoof know so well, the one that has no seasons, that is always full of blood and life, the land you can't see, but you know it's there, like the great harmonic and unyielding skeleton of generation after generation. The true land that sweats its vital juices through the other, the one beasts smell with winnowing nose, the land *campesino* plows search for, the land that can't be pawed by the wind, so unfaithful and useless, such a vagabond.

There in the north, the *provinciano* doesn't surrender the way the coconut palm doesn't surrender in cold regions.

Man is the same as the ground he stands on. Inside, under his skin and hair, is his true form, his true self, disguised in his love of habits and in his life of indolence. A man complete, passionate, jubilant, daring, belligerent, wrapped up in a worn-out and contorted semblance. A man of the land on the inside with another man of land on the outside, with a different vitality, a different form, the one who seems soft though he is covered with edges and joints, who seems deceived when he is deceiving, who doesn't live behind fences but out on the horizon. Under his modulated and deformed language—his Spanish seems to have found the ritual forms very dry—he whistles and speaks with a twang, modulated like an echo on his plains, miserable like the wind when it is bored playing alone on the savanna.

I have seen sunny afternoons on the high plains of my land.

But if I had seen only trees moored eternally by their umbilical cord to the land's womb, if I had seen only carts writing songs on the road, if I had seen only roofs of the little houses and the *campesinos* in their Sunday best wandering idly in the ditches along the road, I would not have seen the meaning of my land.

If I had seen only that, I would have seen nothing.

There is no way to see what my land means. You have to hear it.

You have to close your eyes, some afternoon, any afternoon, from the time the sun is raging up in the sky, until night falls . . . and then, listen.

There is a voiceless murmur at first, brilliant, vibrant afterward, that grows, stuck to the earth. There are thousands of voices. Myriads of screeches; it isn't the sound of the trees or the rivers; it isn't the human voice. It's the cicadas.

Their voices grow under the green, in the dust, in the gardens. They move the leaves, stir the river, build forever and ever, as if they were never going to end, maddening, in waves surging from the ground, fanning down from the houses, forever and ever and ever . . .

Their shrill sound, sharp, a single chord paying with their life for the crime of singing. Hysterical, afflicted, they sing until they burst from being stubborn, foolish, devoted to their singing . . . Until one explodes, extending musical obsession beyond all boundaries, there are myriads, piles of cicadas that drown out any complaint of agony, that will sing until they in turn burst, spent, fulfilling their duty, with a fury, crazed and delirious.

And they die, many die, and there will always be many more to follow, singing incessantly, constantly, never stopping.

The cutting screech, unpleasant, but musical, grows dense under the trees. The pores of the immobile plants seem to shout, and that cry runs from one place to another, from one region to another, covering, leaving the jungle to invade inhabited places, the *campesino*'s house, the road, the cattle ranch, the coffee plantation. It is a single throat with a single note that vibrates and sets things to vibrating. It doesn't vary at all, it is hopelessly foolish and hopelessly insipid and mocking. I have felt it choking me or lulling me to sleep on any afternoon.

If you are passing through, the way you would pass through the countryside, you probably wouldn't hear the voice of the cicadas; the voice would stay behind, useless and resonant. But suddenly you might notice it: you could have been there many hours inside the note, swimming in it and not hearing it, unless the note grabbed you, but in an instant your ear is alert and the note manifests itself at the peak of its delirium, its scream, its resonance; at a peak that seems to have another peak inside, and that same note, without changing, seems higher, more vibrant, tenser, like a cord strained to infinity, like a wave surging on a land of tides and tempests. And suddenly you notice it, wrapping up and smothering your senses.

You are just ears open to the vibration of the countryside. You can't touch it, or see it, or feel it, you can only hear the amazement growing, from amazement to anguish, anguish to pain, pain to drowsiness, until you are cataleptic, by now you hear nothing and you know nothing, you only listen, listen, listen . . .

Translated by Pamela Carmell

Pastor's Ten Little Old Men

Carmen Lyra

WHEN THE LITTLE GIRL saw the newspaper photograph of the perpetrator of the bloody crime that was doubly
sensational because of the victim's being who he was, she was
very sad. The first thing she thought of was Pastor's feet, with
their toes misshapen from life's hard trails. She seemed to see
them, lined up like mutts along the sole of the peon's rough
sandals. Within a family, no one is aware of the secret feelings of the children, even less when the parents are involved
in momentous business dealings, to say nothing of the count-
less duties demanded by high social rank.

The little girl had met the peon during a vacation on the coffee
plantation her parents owned in Tres Ríos. She was wandering one afternoon around the back patio beneath the alders
and eucalyptus trees while her parents and her brothers and
sisters devoted themselves to the distractions distinguished
persons seize upon during outings in the country. To her
childish mind, this patio held a special enchantment, because
she found wonderful places to sit among the tree branches and
spin fantasies, because the wind got tangled among the leaves

like a skein of silk in the paws of a playful cat, because the eucalyptus trees dropped seeds that looked like little hats that she could play with for hours on end, and because watercress grew in the irrigation ditch that flowed through there and small wild ducks with beautiful feathers splashed in its waters.

That afternoon, a man walked into the child's domain, sat down on the grindstone where all the peons sharpened their machetes, took off his sandals, and began to wash his feet. As he scraped away with a scrap of tile, he carried on a conversation with them. "Are you weary, old men? This poor old fellow's still sore because I haven't been able to get out the mangrove splinter he picked up in Puntarenas."

The little girl watched, puzzled. This was a new peon, one she didn't know. If someone had asked her whether he was young or old, she would have answered that he was old, because to children all adults are old. But she never forgot that man with the sturdy limbs and very black eyes and very white teeth gleaming in skin dark as a fired brick.

The girl walked over to the man and asked, "Who are you talking to?"

He answered, dropping his s's the way people from Guanacaste do. "Well, I was talking to these 'old men' here," and he pointed to his toes.

The child's imagination was piqued.

"And they understand you?"

"Sure they understand me," and he stuck his toes straight up in a line, like a row of soldiers awaiting a command.

He had large blackened feet like tree roots. Muscles and veins stood out beneath the skin like knotted hemp, and the nails of his crooked toes made her think of little masks. They reminded her of the small stone idols that came from Indian burial grounds, like the ones her sister had on a shelf in her office. She felt a strong sense of compassion for the two large, ugly feet with the rows of toes like little old men or tiny grotesque animals. The truth is that the girl was a fanciful creature. Chica, the young maid who had always looked after her, had come upon her one night in the corridor as she was placing rags and newspapers over the plants that adorned the wood cutout of a black servant everyone used for an ashtray. She said it was so he wouldn't be afraid or get cold.

The little girl removed her delicate shoes and fine stockings, and compared the man's feet to her clean white ones with pearly heels and tiny plump toes like coral-beaked doves.

The peon said, "Not much alike, are they, child? Yours live like flowers inside those pretty little shoes. Mine, on the other hand . . . From the time I was a little thing like you, my feet have traveled rocky and muddy roads. This toe here was snakebit years ago. It's been half-silly ever since. I almost died. Luckily, I knew to chew three plants that work against snake venom. A secret a Miskito half-breed taught me." That part was a fib, because what really saved him was Butantan serum. But that's how *campesinos* are; they like to make up whoppers about snakes. Half of another toe was missing. It had been lopped off when Pastor was chopping trees for a sawmill up in the mountains. What had he used that time? Mud. Mud and spiderwebs are very good for open wounds. A man he worked with had cut off *all* the toes on one foot. To stanch the blood, he'd bound it with a large leaf filled with mud.

"And what did the toes do?" the girl asked.

The man searched for them in the underbrush, gathered them up in a kerchief like birds' eggs, knotted it, and took them with him.

"And then?"

"Well, he always limped, but as for the rest, his foot healed."

The man and the girl talked until night fell. In the grass, crickets were painting patches of music in the silence. Overhead, the stars were coming out without making a sound. Why was it a person couldn't hear them coming?

The man told the girl, pointing to the constellation of Orion high on the horizon, "Look, child, you see that bunch of stars? Well, that's the four gold nails holding a deerskin set to dry in the sun."

"Who put it up there?"

"Uh . . . You sure have a lot of questions for a little girl."

Chica, the maid, called her. It was getting too late to be out in the night air. And what was she doing barefoot? "God help me, what am I going to do with this crazy girl!"

The very next afternoon, the little girl looked for the peon, who after the day's chores had come to rest beside the banks of the irrigation ditch. Sitting on the grindstone, he was smoking his pipe, and smoke was swirling around his head like a halo shining in the rays of the setting sun. The gentle afternoon breeze stirred the branches of the eucalyptus and alder trees, and twilight was spreading a violet veil over La Carpintera hill. At the water's edge, the ducks were drowsing, standing on one foot with their heads tucked under their bright feathers. The man sat very still, his eyes staring into the distance. The little girl, who was straddling a tree branch, called to him: "Psst, psst."

The man looked up and touched the brim of his hat respectfully.

"What's your name?"

"Me? My name's Pastor."

"Shall I come down so your toes," she pointed to his feet, "can tell me more things, like yesterday?"

"What do you say, old men? You hear what the child wants?" Pastor said, addressing his toes.

His toes sprang up like puppets and wiggled in sign of agreement. "The girl can come down, she won't have to beg."

So the fanciful little girl climbed down and sat in the grass before Pastor and listened to the adventures the ten "old men" had lived once when they'd gone turtle fishing on the beaches of Tortuguero. What could you expect of a child like this little girl, who spent all day wandering along the irrigation ditch or perched among the tree branches? She wanted to know where the water came from and where it went, and she loved it when the wind rocked her in the branches. She talked with the water and talked with the wind. So why should it be strange that she understood the toes of a peon who had wandered all over Costa Rica?

During that summer while the formal members of the family entertained themselves with their bridge, ping-pong, and basketball games, and other important diversions, the girl sought out Pastor, who had fallen into the habit of taking his rest on the grindstone by the edge of the water. Other peons gathered there, too, and children who lived on the plantation; they formed a circle around our Pastor, who had a gift—once he decided to break his long periods of silence— for telling the adventures that had happened to him during his wanderings around the country, and he had fairy tales and ghost stories, as well. The wind whispered in the feathery branches of the alders, and the water flowed away, murmuring so softly that you would have thought it was a sound spun to weave silence. The late-evening song sparrows were courting, and their trilling was to the ears what meadow flowers are to the eyes. From the stable came the warm mooing of cows trying to sort out the bleat of their calves, and all the beauty of the countryside rose toward the luminous sky. All of this was to have a great influence on the little girl's life. The velvety sounds of those summer evenings with La Carpintera

hill's violet hues and Pastor's stories of reality and fantasy
deposited in the depths of that childish soul a sediment of
poetry that later rose into the light of her consciousness, was
diluted in her thoughts, and sketched upon her life a course
different from the one that the unimaginative minds of her
parents would have wished for her. In her imagination, Pastor
and his toes blended together, and for her his stories were a
chorus formed by those shiny, ugly little creatures peeping
out the edge of his sandals. She had given each toe a face
and a name, and she felt a great fondness for them, as if each
were equal to Pastor himself. She wanted to protect them,
as she had wanted to protect the flowerpots and the black
wood servant in the corridor. Later, many years later, when
the little girl moved into the world of adults, she wrote some
delightful stories that were very successful with children and
with simple-hearted adults. They were about adventures in
which the protagonists were "Pastor's Ten Little Old Men,"
toes that had trekked all across Costa Rica. Children learned
to know and love their country through these stories in which
geography, economics, and politics shed all traces of the ped-
antry and boredom so often imposed by official curricula and
instead were humanized and filled with charm.

What things Pastor's toes told the little girl on the *finca!*
Those toes that sometimes recalled a row of soldiers in battle
and, other times, draft horses harnessed to their wagons, had
wandered and roamed through all of Costa Rica. They told
the little girl about a time when Pastor was just a tadpole
and he had gone diving during pearl season in the Gulf of
Papagayo, a body of water with a bad reputation. It was in the
Golondrinas Islands, famous for their banks of oysters. Pastor
recounted it with pride. We were natural divers; none of us
used those clumsy, heavy diving suits. We went down naked

as God had brought us into the world, with nothing but a knife in one hand to cut away the shells stuck to the rocks and to defend ourselves against sharks and rays. We did that six hours every day. The little girl could not imagine what it was like to sink to the depths of the sea to harvest a hundred pounds of pearl oysters. And all the time in the water, you had to hold your breath; minutes were as long as hours.

"Were there lots of pearls?" the little girl asked.

Pastor told her that sometimes days went by without finding a single pearl. But he also found beautiful ones in iridescent oysters, like flowers in a garden, worth hundreds of pesos: pearls white as milk, rosy pearls, a rose like the summer dawn, and gray pearls like gray herons. Had she seen gray herons? Yes, in Parque Bolívar. Immediately Pastor's fantasy came into play, creating palaces and treasures he had seen in the deep waters of the Gulf of Papagayo.

Then he told her about the coasts of Culebra Bay; the foreigners wanted that for their own, because they say that you could maneuver the entire U.S. fleet there, and it was as sheltered from the wind as the big parlor in the little girl's house. There, at night, when you walked on the beach, your feet turned red as fire and oars streamed light instead of water, but a greenish fire and greenish light like the shine off a beetle. Pastor also told about cattle ranches he had seen in Guanacaste, and about the hard work in the rice paddies. You should see the grains, child, so white and pretty, and what they cost! It was almost like harvesting pearls from the bottom of the sea. There's a saying that goes, *rice needs a sky of fire and water for soil*, and that's how it was. "These," he added, pointing to the little old men of his feet, "they know what it is to be deep in mud, cutting rice, and they also know what it is to have the chaff rub your skin raw as you lug three-hundred-pound sacks on your back along unbelievable paths." Yes, the "little old men" knew what it is to cross a mountain in the banana regions of the Atlantic, stuck in clumsy, soaking-wet leather boots and about the infections caused by the noxious mud the Reventazón River leaves behind when it floods; they knew, too, what it meant to cling to the blazing deck of a ship, chasing tuna in the Gulf of Nicoya, gripping the planks to keep from ending up in the jaws of sharks when you're hauling in a hundred-pound fish or throwing out five hundred yards of net.

The child listened to Pastor wide-eyed, and as she listened, she learned that her people were not a slothful people, and she learned the dark conditions under which they had drawn so much wealth from the land and the sea.

What Pastor's "old men" never told the girl was Pastor's own tragedy during a strike in the banana groves. A Yankee from the Banana Company had stolen his wife from him; they'd burned his house, and his two-year-old son had died, charred beyond recognition. That was when he had gone to work on the coffee plantations of Turrialba, and then those on the *Meseta Central*. And finally he'd reached the plantation of Tres Ríos. For Pastor, it was like the Colombian song says:

> *My dogs have all died,*
> *My hut's bare inside,*
> *When I die tomorrow*
> *It's all gone but sorrow.*

Time went by. The little girl was taken back to the city. Pastor kept wandering. The girl often thought of the stories of Pastor's "old men," and wished she could see him again.

Pastor found work in the area of Parrita, which had become the property of a banana company. Maybe the resentment he carried in his heart, as well as life in that green hell where native workers were treated like beasts by the foreigners, led him to do what he did. He was among those who crossed the savage mountains and worked in the deadly swamps on the delta of the Térraba River. He slept in the stinking camps the United Fruit Company crowded the peons into and quenched his terrible thirst with filthy water; he lived for months on end on nothing but beans and bad rice; he survived fevers, lying on wet ground without a roof over his head; and he listened to foreigners insult him at the slightest excuse. During construction on the dock at Quepos, his back and his feet were nothing but raw sores from unloading creosoted railroad ties.

Well, what happened was that one day Pastor shot a gringo, twice, and killed him. People who were there said the foreigner had insulted a poor woman who had just gotten off a boat with her little ones, looking for her husband. Didn't the bitch know that women were forbidden on the site? She hadn't known how to defend herself against the "Mister" who was threatening her, as her children wept and clung to her skirts. The newspapers published the photograph of the "criminal" and the victim, and said that Pastor had acted under the influence of alcohol and subversive ideas.

Pastor was as solitary as a *pizote;* he didn't have many friends. A few people went to visit him during his first months in prison. Then he just disappeared, swallowed up by the justice system. Only the little girl of a wealthy family cried for him at night beneath the covers, when no one could see her. One evening, her mother heard sobs coming from the children's room, and as she pulled on her glove, she peered in at the door, her hair artistically arranged.

"Who's crying?" she asked.

"It's Soledad," came a small voice from one of the beds.

"What's the matter, Soledad?" her mother asked from the hall.

No one answered.

"Is something hurting?"

Silence.

The father appeared, smoothing his tuxedo jacket.

"What's going on?" he asked.

"Soledad's crying about something."

"What's the matter with her?"

"I asked, but she didn't answer."

"She must have a stomachache. She eats too many sweets. She needs a dose of salts . . . "

And the mother and father left, trailing a cloud of distinguished perfume.

It should be told that both of them were thrilled by spiritualism, and that when their social obligations allowed, they attended sessions in which a woman acting as a medium summoned the spirits, who then entered her as slick as a whistle. The girl's parents were particularly interested in the spirits of the dead, and they held long conversations about them with other aficionados. On the other hand, they weren't the least curious about the souls of the living. As far as they were concerned, their children, their servants, their peons, even their friends, might just as well not have *had* souls.

The child cried a long time before she fell asleep. She thought about Pastor locked up in a cell. Chica had told her that they lock criminals in cells like long, narrow rooms. She thought about the toes of his feet, and she seemed to see them lying there, free, dreaming of roads they would never travel again.

Translated by Margaret Sayers Peden

A Leaf of Air

Joaquín Gutiérrez

A LEAF OF AIR, a grand dream from which are born other smaller dreams and from these, others even smaller, until we come to the last of all, the tiniest, which is where the wind begins. That is what my life is like, old friend, like a leaf of air.

I got bored one day and went to Mexico. Costa Rica was very small, as no one knows better than you, and it still is; but when we were young in this postage-stamp country, it was hard to find someone for a little back-and-forth. I mean, you couldn't find a partner, someone who could discuss or exchange ideas, who could talk about Vivaldi or Vallejo. That's the sort of thing I enjoy, as you might expect. And my wanting to be an actor just made it worse. Imagine! There wasn't even a puppet theater, much less a playwright, in the whole country!

Obviously you're screwed, living like that. The years drag along like cripples while a person is eaten away by unsatisfied desires, restless urges, the longing to do something. You were different. Remember, I was still a member of the Anti-Fascist League and was taking some classes, but we're not all born with the stuff to be martyrs or prophets, and besides (to cut the crap), I just couldn't stand to have the mothers hold me up as a bogeyman every time the whores sat down to eat their soup. I wanted to be an actor, that's all, just an actor . . .

But why do you insist that I tell you my story? It's hardly epic or exemplary, it doesn't revolve around any obvious hero like those stories you seem to favor. What a modest tale mine is! A poor deluded man who wanted to be an actor in order to say on stage what he couldn't in everyday life, to shake up, to rile, those fat little couples who are the only ones who can afford to go to the theater. After all, we're not talking about a huge success, interviews everywhere, tours. No, what moonshine! I was resigned to much less.

Obviously, I would never have decided to leave if it hadn't been for what happened with Theresa and the leaf she gave me. I can tell from your face that you don't know what I'm talking about. They grow in Cartago, on little bushes. But this particular one is an old memory. I was seven years old, sick with malaria, and Papa decided we should spend a week someplace cold. Our hotel looked like a castle, with windows set into the tiled walls and two towers that were crowned with weathervanes, red roosters turning in the wind. I was completely bored because I didn't have any friends there, but the night before we left, there was a party for the guests; we were served ice cream, the owner recited a merengue by Amado Nervo with music by Schubert in the background, and afterward came the announcement that her little girl was going to dance. I don't know where she came from, perhaps she'd been spending the summer with her grandmother, because that was the first I had seen of her. The tables were pushed back and then a vision in blue appeared: I thought it was Pinocchio's Blue Fairy, but she was so tiny, I decided she must be the Fairy's baby daughter. I hardly need to tell you, I was overcome with romantic feeling. She was wearing a very short filmy dress and patent-leather shoes, and her hair hung down in ringlets, and when she started to dance, I really thought I was in a castle. When she twirled around she looked like a cloud of spun sugar, like the cotton candy turned out by a machine, except that this cloud was blue, not pink.

The next day at breakfast she asked if I wanted to play with her. We started up a dirt road hand in hand, but she ran more easily than me, so that when I was still climbing the hill, she was already in a field looking for something.

"This is an *hoja de aire*, a leaf of air," she said as she gave it to me. "Hang it by a thread where there is a wind and watch the tiny breezes being born."

It was a big glossy leaf, and I kept it inside my shirt, and when we got to the train a black woman with several baskets let me look out the window, and then I watched as the Castle with its red roosters began to move, faster and faster, and as the clouds rushed past it, until finally it was hidden by a tall house, and when it came out from behind the house, I didn't see it anymore.

That afternoon, as soon as we got back to Limón, I hooked the leaf to the patio door and in a few days each of its smallest lobes had sprouted a minuscule little bush, with tiny roots and all, and I climbed up to look at it and saw that its pretty green color was gradually fading as blemishes started to dot it. Then it occurred to me how terrible it was to have to feed so many little leaves while living only on air, and I took a razor and cut it back to a single leaf that would grow stronger, and I hung it up again, and even then it managed to produce another shoot smaller than itself, but when I came back from school it was gone. The wind must have carried it off.

Now that you know the story, it's true, isn't it? That was the leaf of air I mentioned, the one that carried me off with it.

About my years in Mexico, what can I tell you? Look, as far as they're concerned there are only Mexicans, Spaniards, and gringos in the world, and if you're not a Mexican, pal, they give you some pretty suspicious looks. They have a good reason for it, I won't deny it, with their history, but it's still not very comfortable. I finally managed to get into the University Theater in Guanajuato, but I only got one important part, and that was thanks to the three main actors being sidelined simultaneously with an attack of appendicitis, a death, and a divorce. It was the biggest stroke of luck I ever had in my life. Afterward, it was back to crumbs from the feast, playing an officer in a Casona farce or a husband in *Los Habladores*. So, to make a long story short, after three years of working as an actor there, poor deluded actor that I was, I found myself thrown out one day, just thrown out into the street, on the corner of Alhóndiga. We had to give a gala performance for some bigwigs, and at the last minute they told me that I wasn't going to go on because I still had too strong an accent, so they were making me the prompter. I saw red, but I hid it. It was an incredible potboiler, and in the second act, at the height of the suspense, before the adulterer had been revealed, I gave them a jolt like the one they'd given me—I stopped whispering. You understand? I pretended to be reading, but I was just working my jaws, without making a sound, like this . . .

At first they just looked daggers at me, but by a certain point I had them all around me stretching their necks, with me still moving my mouth, very serious, as if everything was perfectly normal. Why am I kidding you? Clear down to my butt I was shaking with glee. Finally, the leading lady, who played a sweet young thing, called me a son of a bitch, and the entire audience burst out laughing, and then followed that with stamping and yelling, until finally the main characters made a great show of indignation. I tried to explain that this kind of thing sometimes happened, these sudden attacks of laryngitis, that one time in the middle of his sermon the priest in my village . . . It didn't calm them down. They wanted to lynch me, and in fact, they did throw me out. And that's not all. The state governor said that if I ever set one of my miserable feet in Guanajuato again, that he would personally "shoot me."

What could I do? I went back to Mexico City, to Pocitos, my street, and I had to make a living, old friend. Because in other parts of the world remarkable things were happening: the Russians had traveled across the Milky Way, the Pope had been unable to swallow the Pill, and the Vietnamese had upset the Yankees. What a marvelous world we live in. But as for me, such wonderful things didn't happen to me, and they still hadn't come up with any way to stay alive without having to eat every day. And there was Infantina, besides, who ate more and worked less than me. Her real name was Abundia, but she liked to be called Infantina. It was no great romance, I swear it. After Theresa, I couldn't fall in love with anyone else, but that didn't mean Infantina and I weren't good together. "Sell car insurance," she told me, without turning off the radio, listening to those Mexican soap operas that would make a dead man weep. I sold insurance, I did a lot of things. In fact, what didn't I do? My most colorful job—performing with a circus. It was a way to make the most of my experience as an actor, the power of the boards, sure, but most important, the circus offered us both jobs, and that way Infantina wouldn't have to sit home with nothing to do but listen to soap operas and think about our neighbor. I took the job, a little humiliated, but I took it.

It was simple: pow! a big slap in the face, throw myself backwards, spin on my head, and when I started to get back up, pow! a good one on the other cheek. The children went crazy laughing, and that was the only thing, because my pay—you can imagine! I was also in charge of cleaning out the cages—only the elephant filled a pail—and working in the ticket booth.

Infantina was happy herself. They made a sequin costume for her, it revealed her terrific legs, and her career was launched: she went from magician's to horse-trainer's assistant—which meant a ten-peso raise—then to manager's secretary, then trapeze artist's mistress, and finally became whore to the whole troupe.

Pow, take that, keep on dreaming!

I came to blows with several of them, but when she started to make sweet eyes at the weight lifter, I reached my limit and gave up on her. And the years took a slide: I went downhill so fast it still makes my head spin.

Of course, I was sad to leave her. We had gotten used to living together, she sewed my buttons on, we did a smooth tango in bed, and when I found myself in my garret, sitting in my chair, alone again, I thought: life is a bitch . . . That's the truth, whether you've got five hundred or five thousand! And the worst thing, probably the worst thing, is that right after all that, I started thinking of Theresa more and more.

Because I had seen her again, many years later, in Limón. One day I saw her mother going into a house, and I sat waiting in the gutter, with a peculiar feeling here, in my chest, until she finally appeared, holding her father's hand, wearing knee socks and dressed in white. At home later I learned that their hotel had burned down, and then one day we bumped into each other on the wharf. I suggested that we go for a dip, she didn't know how to swim, and—look, old friend, do you see these hands?—well, it is so easy: I close my eyes and I feel her on each fingertip, I'm not lying to you, on each fingertip, when I held her up so she could float, and a wave came, and she was frightened and grabbed me around the neck.

Oh! Why, it was like a dream, or better yet, like a bubble. A bubble that popped on the horrible day of the lizards.

That was the afternoon she called to me from her window. Her parents were out. She took my hand and led me to the patio. It was huge, with two mangoes and a fig tree. And I remember, as if I could still see them, a parrot on a perch and lots of clothes stretched out to dry.

"Yes, it is nice," Theresa agreed, "but there are too many lizards."

She was afraid of them. She believed that they grew up to become dragons. When I told her that I knew how to capture them alive, she gave me a kiss on the cheek, and then you should have seen me poking my head among the tree roots! Before long we had five of them in a bottle, pretty things, with spines like sunflowers. Theresa found them lovely, until she suddenly got a very odd expression, as if she were squinting.

"We have to kill them," she said to me in a serious voice. "Let's fill the bottle with vinegar."

"No," I said, lying, "vinegar wouldn't bother them at all; lizards' milk is just like vinegar; they're used to it."

Then she suggested we throw a lit match into the bottle, or else throw them into the sea, but since the critters hadn't done anything to me, I raised objections to everything, and she went into the house without a word and came back with a hot-water bottle.

"Now you'll see," she said, pouring the lizards into the hot-water bottle. Then she screwed the top down tight: "Touch them."

It was exciting to feel them moving around inside there. She pressed the bottle against her little chest and it made her laugh, but after that she went back to her demands, insisting and insisting until she got her way. We piled up dry leaves and papers, we hung the bottle from a branch of the mango tree, we lit the fire and squatting, choking on the smoke, we watched fascinated as the flames began to lick at the bottle, until all of a sudden one side of the rubber puffed up into a ball, the dark red turned a pale pink, almost transparent, and the light shining through revealed the silhouettes of the lizards inside moving about frantically. At last the ball burst open and at the hole one terrified lizard appeared, its small tongue out, and it fell into the fire and was burnt to a crisp, and then the others too, one after another, and only the last one got away, making an Olympic leap and disappearing among the roots.

I thought Theresa had gone mad when she first started to scream. Next she burst into tears, and then she started to hit me, pounding my head and neck with her darling little fists, while she kept up her wailing, the bottle belonged to her mother, and what was she going to do now? I managed to calm her down finally, and I started to caress her, and I swore I would steal a bottle from my house and no one would know and, me caressing her all the while, we moved under the fig tree, and she was just taking off her panties when in walked her mother. I got out by the skin of my teeth, but they gave Theresa quite a beating and forbade her to see me ever again.

From that day on I dreamt about her. I saw her dancing dressed in blue, and as she passed in front of me, she drew a lizard from the front of her gown and threw it in my face. Other times she'd be running, knives with legs following her in hot pursuit, and I wanted to come to her rescue, but the Indians had tied me to the track, and the train was coming. I had one dream even worse: the door would open suddenly and a strange masked figure would appear; it stuck out its tongue at me, the tongue turned into a flame, and the flame started to chase me.

These nightmares came back to me in Mexico. Every night. Always the same. Although from time to time I also had other, more pleasant dreams, about the third time we met.

We were much bigger when I saw her one afternoon at a carnival. I tell you, from the minute we met, we might as well have been magnetized! We went on all the rides together, the merry-go-round, the ferris wheel, the bumper cars. Squeezed into a gunnysack on the slide, as if by accident I touched her breasts. It was so wonderful, it made me dizzy! Later, in the Haunted House, we experimented with kissing, ignoring the hairy spiders and the skeletons and the other kids screaming all around us, and thus began a grand passion, one of those that comes with shivers, the kind that can't be described because there are no words. It was Juliet, and Daphnis and Chloë, and Anna Karenina and Othello and Sulamita. All of them, all together! It was joy, but more than a joy, it was a frenzy, as if we were gasping for breath, as if we were going to die of pure happiness!

And I remembered all this, sitting alone in my shabby chair, staring at the rusted tin roofs outside my garret window. I had forgotten how to eat, and my belly button was starting to stick to my spine. Because I tell you, Quincho, after the circus I started to go hungry. Ah, yes, you'd better believe me, old friend. Hungry and out of luck. Ochas died, the only one who came to see me sometimes and gave me a couple of pesos. But of course, you'd remember him. Anyway, he died. One night he came home after a few drinks, lay down in bed with a cigarette, and set the mattress on fire. Fortunately, I didn't hear about it in time because I wouldn't have been able to bear to see him; they said he looked awful. I went to the funeral, but what a funeral it was: the widow, two little girls, white-faced and weeping, and an old woman. It was April and, between the long walk and the fresh air, I worked up a ferocious appetite, but I didn't dare. How could I ask them for something! I gave them my regrets, very solemn and sad, because that's how I really felt, and I went back to my room yet again.

It feels lousy to go hungry, doesn't it? But you, you've never felt it. Yes, I suppose so, I believe you, but not like mine. Sure, every once in a while I got a little work, conning tourists in Lagunilla or helping out a foot doctor—there are careers for everybody, right?—or doing horoscopes, but none of these jobs lasted very long. Fear had gotten into me again, like a twinge, or a prickling on the inside. Maybe a psychiatrist could have explained it, but I didn't understand it at all, and I don't know how to tell you about it. I was committed for a while and when I came out I was better. Basically, I think that what cured me was the shock alone, seeing what a zoo it was inside. But, after all, it was a sickness like any other and no reason to panic, isn't that true? Some people have trouble with their lungs, others with their prostates. Thinking, remembering: that's what made me sick.

I'll get to the point: one day, after I don't know how many years, opportunity knocked. A friend with a car offered to drive me, and there were several people who would have jumped at the offer because, I tell you, at the Consulate they never wanted to listen when I asked them to send me back home.

From Managua I had to get here on the bus. I sold every-thing I owned, all the things I loved most: my chair—the bed wasn't mine—my complete Shakespeare, the Greeks, Stan-islavski's *Method*. Things that even in my worst moments, I had never been willing to get rid of. I gave my friend a couple of pesos for gasoline because, I tell you, friends who don't want you to pay for the gasoline you won't find in this world, and I didn't have enough for the bus. Three dollars I think it was, a pittance, but you know how hard it is to get three dol-lars together when all your belongings—your worldly goods, as the lawyers say—have been reduced to a pair of flannel pants, a chocolate brown jacket so big I was swimming in it, a pair of shoes, and a shirt. What would you sell, tell me? The shoes? And make your return to your fatherland, prodigal son, with your tootsies bare? The pants, then? And step off the bus on Avenida Central covering your balls with a news-paper? No, no, I had an out: to go look for the Infantina. She was well-heeled, a silver-plated fox, gold-lamé suit, and since she was quick and maybe still liked me a little, she caught on as soon as I opened my mouth, and she came through, and besides giving me three dollars, managed to feed me for the next two days like I hadn't eaten for years. So well that I was laughing to myself as I went down the street! It meant I didn't have to come home looking like a famine victim, right?

The trip proved quite useful: it was as if I left behind all my dirty laundry, as if I'd heaped it into a mountain and set it on fire. I was going back to my own country; it was March and I knew that when I got there the coffee trees on the hillsides and the oaks on the savanna would be in bloom. At last I'd be breathing fresh air again, after so many years breathing the foul air of that Aztec, Olmec, or Tontonac metropolis. And you're surprised that I say it's foul? Then listen to me, they went so far as to put me in jail. That was when I was working as a cabdriver, and one Sunday I was going to Chapultepec, driving slow, and I saw a couple arguing; she gave him a push, and without looking where she was going ran into my side window. It was nothing, but she was pretty, so I offered to take her to have it looked at. They handed me over to the police. The doctor had already made the report, but they made him put down a concussion. Ah, those sons of bitches! They did it just to scare me, understand? But how was I supposed to give them a bribe if I didn't have a dime? Then they charged me with another accident, where the guy had all his bones broken, and shut me in the slammer. Eight days I was there and you should have seen the fortune Infantina had to pay before they let me out. Afterward she told me she had pawned a ring and I believed her, but later I thought about the business with the circus, and I'm sure I understand it all: that was when things went sour for her, poor thing.

But, I tell you, during my trip I felt like I had washed and ironed my soul and put some starch in it. Because people are capable of resurrections like that. A man breaks out of the tomb and the stink lasts only a little while. Lazarus. Who would have had the nerve to say anything to Lazarus a week later? Sure, picture this: "Hey, Lazarus, why don't you put on some deodorant." Nope, no one would have been able to say something like that. No one!

Luckily my friend, the one with the car, didn't talk very much, so I traveled through all of Central America with my window open, thinking and enjoying the warm air. And as we got closer and closer to my sweet homeland, I started to get silly and began to sing patriotic songs: "Attack, attack, under a steady rain of bullets, our fire will not die . . ." You remember it? And when my friend kidded me, asking since when gunshots have raised such a passion in anyone, I swore that if he kept it up I was getting out of the car.

I said good-bye to him in Managua, spent the night on a bench in the park everyone calls the Somoza Hilton, and the next day I picked out a window seat on the bus. Liberia, Palmares, Alajuela. We're almost there already, idiot, don't collapse in tears now. Then Heredia, just like I left it. Some old ladies got on there with some turkey cocks. And the Puente del Virilla and Cinqo Esquinas and finally, the bus depot.

When I got off the bus to walk down Avenida Central, my knees felt like wet noodles. Almost twenty years away, that's nothing to sneeze at, right? I didn't even look at the young people, the whole generation born since I left, who couldn't know me, or me them, but I stopped and stared at every bald guy, at every graybeard, at every person bent over with rheumatism, to see if I recognized anyone. The first one was Snakefarts, as we called him, do you remember? Because he was so slippery. How he'd aged, his face had fallen down, as if it had been built by an amateur carpenter. Anyway, he tried to be nice and invited me for a cup of coffee. When he held his cup, his hands shook. What was it? Alcohol, that's what. He'd been a heavy drinker for years, with pink elephants riding bicycles, the whole show. Then, and this is how he put it, he'd reformed, and now he was working guarding the bosses in labor disputes. And for that he'd reformed. The wretch.

I put up with it and went on listening. And I tell you, I put up with it, although you may find it hard to believe me, because I've never given up some of the ideas we had when we were boys. I will do everything else and be everything else, before I will cut myself off from them. And I was thinking all this while Snakefarts went on and on with the tale of his half-life, until he finally realized that he'd been the only one talking and asked about me. So I made up a story, in Cinemascope and living color, about appearing in *Cyrano* with López Tarso and about palling around with Siqueiros.

"Yes," he responded in a sibylline tone, "I knew that after your parents died, you decided to stay in Mexico permanently, but I hadn't heard about what a success you were."

Watch it, OK? I told myself. "And apart from my old man and old lady," I asked him quite seriously, "do I have any other family living here in Costa Rica?"

He gave me an astonished look. "You still have a sister," he said, as if telling me I still had a nose or two eyes.

"Ah, that's right," I agreed with him, "now that you mention it, I remember her."

He almost knocked over his cup, and that was when I realized he'd been trying to escape for quite some time, but I beat him to it; I jumped up and rushed out without telling him good-bye or that I hoped I would never have to see him again for the rest of his shitty little cirrhotic life.

But it left a bitter taste in my mouth. I swear, this first encounter in my homeland left me upset. To cool down, I walked all the way to the Sábana and then back, and I was starting to feel better when just as I was walking past the Church of La Merced, I suddenly felt as if I'd been struck by lightning. A half block away, on the same side of the street, Theresa was walking toward me! She had a girlfriend on one arm and a crocodile bag on the other. More mature, of course, that's natural, but with the same gorgeous eyes and legs as ever. Falling all over myself, I stopped in the middle of the sidewalk to force her to stop, and when she was in front of me and looking at me, I had a terrible feeling. She might as well have knocked me out with a single punch. Do you understand? She didn't seem to realize who I was.

"Theresa," I finally managed to stammer.

"Leave me alone," she said. "Go away or I'll call the police."

I felt as though instead of legs I had mashed bananas. It's true that her voice sounded different—hers was thicker, more velvety—but just in case I followed her to the Rainbow Market and waited outside eating some *nances*, and when they came out her friend flashed me a joking look, and just then a limo pulled up, one of those that are twenty feet long with a kitchen and a TV set, and it swallowed them up and they disappeared down the street.

I stood there awhile until I calmed down, finished eating the *nances*, and I went into a drugstore to use the phone. I tried, but didn't turn up my sister.

"You know the Agüero family?"

"There are several," the pharmacist answered suspiciously. And true, I did have a three-day beard.

"Don Felipe Agüero," I persisted, "although don Felipe is dead, perhaps you know something about his daughter." Since he was still giving me a sour look, I decided to lie: "The reason I'm asking, sir," I told him, "is that I was told that doña Lucinda needs a plumber, but unfortunately I lost her address." It came in handy, see? my old skill as an actor, but the bastard was a smartass, unlikely as that seems in a druggist.

"And when they gave you the address," he asked with a sneer, "did they tell you at the same time that the lady's father was named Felipe and that he was dead?"

There wasn't much I could do. He'd caught me. Improve my pitch for the next time. And still looking at me oddly, he snatched the directory away as if I had the pox, and that made me mad, and I said so to the asshole, including a few words about his dying, and he started to scream, calling for some Eduviges, who was surely the one stirring the permanganate in the backroom, and I left. And look at how things go: thanks to this I suddenly remembered an aunt with the same name, poor silly old biddy, and I called her from a bar and she gave me my sister's address without my even telling her who I was. Why should I go into that, right?

I went over there. I knocked. A cute little house, freshly painted, on Aranjuez. She answered the door herself.

"Hello, Lucinda," I said. "It's me, Alfonso."

She gave a little hiccup. And she wasn't putting it on; she had really believed I was dead. Then we kissed and embraced, and she couldn't stop sobbing while lovely black Helena Rubinstein tears ran down her cheeks. Afterward, still hiccupping, she told me about our parents' death, my father of diabetes, and mama calling "Alfonso" and all sorts of other things, and of course I was really moved, but she insisted on telling me all the details, which kept getting smaller and smaller, and finally I got out the fact that I hadn't had a bite to eat since breakfast the day before and was feeling awfully hungry, and luckily the little light finally went on, and she called the maid and got me *café con leche* and cheese with guava jelly, and they asked if I wanted some eggs, and I said fine, just to be polite, and at last my sister pulled her head out of the icebox—I'd never seen a refrigerator as full of good things—and handed me a big slice of cake with some fruit on top.

She had already stopped crying, but now she seemed quite nervous, as if there was something she wanted to ask me. And I beat her to it and told her that, yes, I had come back broke, without a penny, but if it wasn't any problem, I could sleep on the sofa. Then, looking up at the ceiling, she told me she was married and her husband would be home in a half hour, so maybe I should get cleaned up a little to make myself a bit more presentable.

She lent me everything, fresh razor, hot water, clean shirt and a pair of socks—the next day I saw mine in the garbage—and while I was bathing, she ironed my pants herself and mended a thin spot in the rear end. I dressed up like a dandy and came into the living room just as the brakes screeched outside.

My brother-in-law wasn't hostile to me. Just the opposite. Of course he'd heard a lot about me but, to be honest with me, he too had thought I was dead.

"Good heavens, no," I said, "I'm certainly alive, more alive than ever."

Then I told them about the Aztec ruins and a little bit about Infantina, as if I was a widower or something like that, and I invented a son for them who had died drowning, trying to liven up the tabletalk and distract my brother-in-law from the shots he was taking at me, and at bedtime I settled down on the sofa and thought things over before falling asleep. A life like mine doesn't necessarily make a man cynical, right? I sometimes felt that it did, because that way you protect yourself better than if you just went walking down the street naked, exposing your soul. And yet, the more I thought about it, the more I was sure that everything would work out—all I had to do was find Theresa. Of course, in the meantime I had to work, but I had already heard my brother-in-law say that he owned a factory, and if my salary wasn't too high at first it wouldn't be too long before things started looking up, and I'd have a nice suit made and half a dozen wash-and-wear shirts, and once I was looking good, I'd go out and look for her.

I slept very well that night. I had nightmares, like I always do, but nice ones. With a bit of effort I would be flying a couple of feet off the ground, with people admiring me as I went by. It feels good to be admired, even in your dreams.

I woke up late, the sun high, the house silent. They'd all gone out and I lay lounging on the sofa until I heard singing in the kitchen. I'd noticed her there the day before, a chubby little thing, about twenty years old, with braids and caramel breasts. I opened my brother-in-law's closet and put on his dressing gown, washed, splashed cologne all over myself, and stared at myself in the mirror.

"Alfonso," I said to myself, "what have you done with your life? And yet here you are, wrapped in blue satin!" As soon as I said that though, I was overcome by a terrible sadness, because I realized that I am a good man. Because whether you're good or embittered and cynical often depends on whether you have somewhere to clean up, so that people look at you without distrust, they don't scream and threaten to call the police. Frankly, I've found that it's not that hard to be good. And thinking about all this, I raised the venetian blind, and the sun came into the room like an orange vendor, and there was the servant, attacking the furniture with a feather duster. I don't know what came over me, but the truth is that my heart gave a leap like it sometimes does and suddenly I felt so bucolic, I tore off my dressing gown and stood like that, naked as the day God thrust me into the world, in front of those eyes rich with mint and sugar candy wrapped in tiny orange leaves. What a yell she let out!

Afterward I tried to calm her down, talking through the door to the kitchen, where she had barricaded herself, but since she kept on shrieking I had to threaten that if she said anything to my sister I would put marijuana in her food, and when she was out cold I would come and climb into bed with her. Then she began to pray, and when I heard that, I had a furious desire to sit her in my lap like my little sister and make her feel better by whispering sweet things to her. For that to happen I decided I'd better get dressed and—what luck—I discovered that my brother-in-law's clothes fit me. A little bit tight, but they fit, so that I had some to choose from. I liked this, the English cashmere, and once I put it on, I went out to the patio, and while I was walking around admiring the azaleas, suddenly I saw a lizard running up the garden wall. Which reminded me again of all I had lost, and I was completely out of control, and luckily the maid had taken advantage of my going out on the patio to make her escape, because I swear that if she hadn't, at that moment I could have given her quintuplets at least.

Now I was alone with the entire house at my disposal. I looked for the whiskey and found it (businessmen always have at least one bottle), and I poured myself a big glass. Then another. Then I threw myself down on the sofa with the phone at my side and I looked it up: Goicoechea, Góngora, González—holy shit are there Gonzálezes in this country—and finally, Gómez Theresa. It didn't say widow-of, or wife-of. Nothing, a nice old maid, my friend. I got my butterflies under control and called.

"Hello, yes, little girl, please get your aunt for me. Your aunt isn't there? Ah, then she isn't your aunt"—smart little girls always give me a pain—"And where can I find your mother? In the National Library? Why, does she work there?"

I hung up. Single with a daughter. Fine, what can you do about it? I have paternal feelings too, and I think I would make a wonderful stepfather. And thinking these things, I left the house and saw the maid spying on me from the corner, still frightened. I pretended I didn't see her and took the few blocks to the library almost flying. Where are you, my childhood? I am going to meet you there. And why did I turn my back on you and feign indifference for so many years when at bottom I was still the same sniveling sentimental adolescent who burst into tears reading Geraldy? But does anyone have the right, have any blasted right to keep me from being a sentimental fool? You tell me, Joaquín Gutiérrez, with all your chess and your walrus mustache, does anyone have that right?

In the library there were only three retirees reading ancient journals and in another room some little boys face-down in the adventures of Sandokan. Had Theresa finished her work and left? I was on the point of doing that myself when all of a sudden I spotted her, in a corner, hidden behind dark glasses and a mountain of books. I approached her on tiptoes and sat down in front of her without her seeing me.

"Theresa," I said in a low voice, afraid she might faint.

She pushed the books aside to look at me. "Yes, sir," she said very seriously, as if she hadn't recognized me.

"Theresa," I repeated, "I'm back. After so many years I have finally returned. I think you must have forgiven me by now."

She took off her glasses and I immediately saw that she had green eyes, deep green, like verdigris.

"You are Theresa Gómez, aren't you?" I asked, afraid I'd been misled a second time.

"Yes," she answered. "Why?"

"But you used to have dark eyes . . . "

"That seems unlikely," she told me, starting to smile.

"Unlikely maybe, but not impossible."

"OK, let's say I had black eyes."

She was a devil. And I liked it. I liked the way she played the game. She had a light delivery, nice. I too have always played, as much as I could and, I tell you, it's the best part of life. And then there were her eyebrows, I liked them too, so neat and symmetrical.

"It would be better if we never had to be serious," I said, "but right now I must be."

"How do you know my name?" she interrupted.

"Ah, that's a secret. And I know other things, too, that you are a historian . . . "

"Because you just read the spines of these books . . . "

"But I also know that you have a bright little girl and still use your maiden name, which to me seems like a magnificent gesture of rebellion against convention."

That she didn't like. "It must be some other person with the same name," she said. "And excuse me, I have so much work to do that I must ask you to pardon me."

Saying that, she once more disappeared behind the pile of books.

I stood up at that point so I could see her and I said, in lofty tones: "I am looking for Theresa Gómez, miss; your name was in the telephone book, I called, your daughter answered, and I came to see you. That is all. I realize that I have disturbed you. I have made you lose precious moments from your work, and a few moments of a historian's time are worth many years in the life of a man from the working class . . . "

She just kept right on taking notes without even glancing up, and then I felt that I could no longer conceal my feelings, that I could pretend no more. My God, if I had to see the same ghost, feel the same fear grabbing hold inside like a tiny animal gnawing at my guts and if I had to stand there any longer, I would have been reduced to what I'd been in Mexico, and I walked out, carrying myself like a prince, one foot in front of the other, without looking back at her, not even once, but feeling in my heart like a miserable foolish clown.

I went back home, I can't really tell you why. My sister had already returned from her shopping and had heard about everything. Even the gray suit. And the brilliantine too, I suppose, because I had forgotten to put the cap back on, and her house was appallingly tidy.

The poor thing, for all that, she did what she could.

"Alfonso, listen to me, our apartment is small," she said. "I've been married almost thirty years and I don't want to ruin my happiness. Luis is a very good man, but very methodical, very serious, and he wouldn't understand you. Already last night he said that he could tell you were an intellectual, really different, not like everyone else. That he knew you had lived a lot, and he was afraid that you wouldn't get used to Costa Rica. Add to that what he's going to think now, and you'll understand how hard it would be for you to live with us . . . But come back, come to see me. No, no, don't take it off, keep it. I'll make up some story to tell Luis, that I scorched it while I was ironing. And come back, like I said. If you run into some kind of problem one of these days, come and talk with me about it."

"I only have one problem," I told her with a solemn face. "I have an old wound and my life is oozing away through it." I put it that way because I enjoy being melodramatic sometimes and to see if maybe I could bring back her hiccups. But it didn't work. And she was smiling with relief when she closed the door behind me.

I left feeling rather sad. It was logical. I had discovered that my sister had the same genes as me, but in the opposite order, upside-down, etc. And I wandered around until I came to this bench and then sat down, and you walked past, and I called out to you. That's all. Like I told you at the start, just a life, mine, hardly socialist realism. On the contrary, you who have such a nice way of putting things would say it's pure existentialism, and you'd be right. And now I know you're going to give me a sermon and tell me life is worth living

and tomorrow is another day and all that. And that is exactly
what's worst, that I know you're right, but what am I going to
do, tell me that, what am I going to do?

All right, start talking . . . or take your time if you have
to. I know it's not easy. Two childhood friends run into each
other and one tells his life story, the naked truth, exposing all
the shames and sorrows, and the other has to find something
to say. Come on, Quincho, I want to hear what you have to
say to me. Doesn't anything come to mind?

I looked at Alfonso. On top of everything, I knew a part of his
story that he didn't know. Theresa Gómez—he didn't need to
tell me of their romance because we had all seen it close up
and, I must admit, envied it—had died ten or twelve years
ago. It seemed impossible that Alfonso didn't know, that no
one had written him in Mexico to tell him. I decided not to
pull any punches, to blurt it right out:

"Okay, Alfonso, I'm sorry, but Theresa is dead. Didn't anybody tell you?"

The moments that followed seemed to stretch forever. And
only when the ashes started to fall on my lapel did I finally
dare to look at him. Alfonso was winking and smiling.

"You know, Quincho," I think to myself, "every man is a mess
on the inside. I've just told you about my life, leaving out a
few things, including some pickles. So don't bother trying to
convince me. I know that Theresa is in Cartago. She's looking
out the window set into the tiled wall beneath the red roosters
turning and turning in the wind. And the Castle is moving
away from me, but it's not the Castle that's moving, you know,
it's the train. It's all the same. My life has kept on moving,
but her, no, she is there, and the only thing bad now is that I

don't have money for the bus, and when you walked by I was thinking just that, about going to hock this, they'd have to give me something for it, it's English cashmere, so that I can go to Cartago to see her. What made me hesitate is that I look so elegant in it. You hardly notice that it's a little small on me, right? And because it's been a long time since I looked so elegant, I thought it would be nice to arrive at her house dressed like this. But no, no, no; don't think I'm going to hit you up for a loan. I've always thought you were smarter than that, you understood me better. And deep down there's only one thing I ever really wanted: to be understood, to be understood just a little. You're such a materialist, you should be able to explain it all to me. And don't come telling me that my leaf of air is only a symbol and that symbols don't correspond to any physical reality. Because I know they exist! It's true, Quincho, isn't it? You pick a little leaf, and from each lobe a new plant is born, and they keep getting smaller and smaller, it's true, but you know that there is one infinitely large and another infinitely small, like in Achilles and the tortoise, remember that, back in high school? All you can do is take care of the leaf, especially the last, the smallest, because that is where the wind comes from. See, that's it. But, good grief, we've spent the whole afternoon talking, and I don't want to get to Cartago after dark. I'd like to get there early, to climb the dirt road up the hill as the sun rises, to let myself through the fence at the same pasture where Theresa gave me the leaf and to look for a low branch of a savanna oak that's in full bloom to hang it on . . . And that's the other thing I have to buy when I hock my clothes: some cord, a thick rope. The only thing is, I'd like it to be blue, and I don't know if they sell blue rope."

Translated by Carol Christensen

The Palmitero

Max Jiménez

TALL AND UPRIGHT, with slender trunks, their feathery green tops waving like plumes from the helmets of the oaks and cedars.

When trees are felled on the mountains sometimes the palmetto is spared, and when the mists blow in along the mountain peaks, as if to rekindle sight in a blind man, the great leaves of the palmetto seem to become one with God, to fuse with the phantasmagoria of the clouds turning the color of mother-of-pearl in the dying sun.

The mist covers the landscape again, and the palmetto wraps itself up in its eternal companion.

These are the fan palms, the prey of the palmitero, whose single purpose is to harvest their hearts.

You have to hear the screams as each palm splinters to earth, as it falls on its lifelong sisters on the mountainside. You have to see how each palmetto victim buries itself into the damp soil, perhaps seeking a grave, an honorable grave in the dark earth that has so kindly given it nourishment year after year.

It is deep, it is a bluish black, it is a heart-rending cry, that sound of a trunk splintered in pain, the fall of the palm tree, so wonderfully lithe, towering over its companions to drink in the mist, the rain, and the sun.

The palmitero begins his journey, stuffing about ten palm hearts into his sack, a foot and a half of the only soft part of the palm leaf. With the load strapped to his head, his pants rolled up so the mud won't weigh him down, he comes to a run-down inn, for people with discriminating palates, an inn that fills up during Lent, when palm flesh must substitute for animal flesh among the faithful.

The palmitero is sometimes able to improve his business and a mare is added to his entourage. The mare has a languorous face, her head low, moving between her legs like a pendulum as she goes up and down hills and her hind legs thrust out to hold herself up in the hobbling and slippery mud of the back roads.

Peje was not a palmitero out of conviction or out of love for the arduous treks. He frequently told the story of what had turned him into a palmitero. Such stories are often told, even to those who have no relation at all to anything that happens to us, probably in order to unload on somebody else ideas that are weighing us down, as though looking for a walker stronger than we are to help us carry the load.

So it was that Peje was coming down from the mountain after dropping off some cows that belonged to the owner of a dairy. He was young and it was a long trip. On his way back, with the sun growing dim and a torrential rain coming down, he chanced upon another traveler on horseback. But the horse was wandering over the road, as if it were not being guided at all. The night was disappearing deeper into itself, and Peje spoke to the nearly invisible rider:

"Eh, friend, this time you really tied one on!" But the man didn't reply. "OK, OK, don't talk if you don't feel like it, but at least hold on to the reins."

Peje grabbed the rider's hands and, to his horror, realized they were the hands of a dead man. His vision became sharper, as can happen when fear takes over, and he could clearly see the dead body of a man; it was tied to the saddle with its eyes half-opened in death. Peje saw death, a much greater death, in the dark shadows, where the branches of the trees along the road met each other, where it doesn't rain because the heavens are crying.

Peje spurred his horse but the other followed him. It made no difference to him at all once he reached town that the people told him to calm down, that he was just a man who had died in the woods, and that because there was no one to carry him back, his companions had tied him to the mare and had stayed behind in some bar drinking rum, and that since the horse knew the road, she had just kept going.

It was all useless: the image of that mare of death had engraved itself in Peje's mind. He couldn't sleep, and his eyes bulged out exactly as they do when people see things that no one else sees. "There! There! There it is!" And nobody else sees anything at all.

He began to run away, to move from place to place, and there was no better profession for that than the palmitero's for always being on the move . . .

Sometimes he took his family with him, improvising shelter in the woods, and for months on end no one heard anything from Peje, until his memory would torment him again, and he'd pick up and return.

He'd sell his load of palmettos, buy supplies, and plunge deep into the mountains again, like someone putting his soul in a tunnel looking for oblivion.

Peje was not a thief by nature; he had become used to helping himself to things according to the solitary freedom of the mountain. Before making that trip with the dead man, he had never stolen with the naturalness of a fish that opens its mouth to take in nourishment. Before, he had been called Ezequiel, the son of Señor Santiago. No longer was that almost godlike power of his father any use to him when his father would say with all his paternal authority:

"Don't run away if you haven't done anything wrong. That business with the dead man is over now. I'm your father and if I tell you I don't see anything, it's because I don't."

"Don't say that to me, father; the more you talk about it, the more I see that dead man on his horse, and when those bums in town start asking me if I still see him, I see him even more. So I have to run away."

Peje, with his beard and bulging eyes, growing skinnier by the day, didn't upset anyone with his disappearances, because his father used to say:

"He's like the poor man's dog; he gets lost but he comes back when he's forgotten all about the beating he got."

Peje's periods of absence in the mountain grew longer and longer; and because he went hungry, the rope at his waist made it twice around. He would stay at abandoned palmitero shacks at the edge of the tangled forest, shacks of palmiteros who had disappeared no one knows when, falling into ravines when an embankment gave way, horse and palmitero ending up deep at the bottom of the stream.

Peje plunged deeper and deeper into the perpetual rainfall, into the mud, with his preacher's beard, his eyes like circles of astonishment, feeding on hearts of palm and drinking the tears from the one-eyed rocks lining the steep hills.

Peje did not die. Señor Santiago, his father, continued to wait for him. Peje was disappearing into the arms of the mountain, like the trail of the blue *pajuila* birds in flight . . .

Translated by Gabriel Berns

Here

Louis Ducoudray

MY WIFE AND I sleep face down. We don't have any children. We know everyone sleeps the same way, face down. No
one dares to look at the ceiling, except on Fridays, the day
the men with red pointed hats arrive before dawn to take the
wings away in very long trucks. They bring them back on
Saturday, before sunset. It seems they give the wings a forti-
fied concentrate the Company brings from another country.
We imagine the yard where they feed the wings is enormous.
How else could so many hungry and desperate wings be
accommodated? At ten in the morning, when they've finished
picking them up, and the wings are all together, their fluttering raises a giant cloud of dust that billows up and darkens
the neighborhood for hours, and then falls slowly over the
roofs and seeps between the boards of the walls, through the
cracks, and the dust covers the bedspreads and the floors, and
the cupboards, and our noses. Everything here is soft and
white. We wake up covered with dust.

When the Company started to build their installations
ninety years ago, the first pair arrived inside an airtight metal
case with three locks. A man with a red hat more pointed

than the rest took it off the train and showed it in the plaza. Our parents told us that they were small and tame, two wings joined together without a trunk, without eyes or a head, without feet and without a tail. You could hold them in the palm of your hand. They liked the sweaty warmth, and they were quiet, nestling down there. Through their thin plumage you could see a pink, almost transparent skin, like that of a recently hatched bird. This pair was locked up inside the Company building. They had to take care of it every day, until it could adapt to the climate and whatever might happen. They say that my grandfather tried a thousand times to destroy it—he kicked, he broke the Company's windows; six Sundays he climbed into the pulpit to issue the most serious warnings ever heard, that this was not about some songbird, a bunch of idiots who couldn't see beyond their noses, and until the day a wing struck him and finished him off, he ran tirelessly through the streets, asking for help, covered with scapulars that appeared to sprout from his beard, and ringing a zinc pail like a bell to keep everyone alert. But since he had the reputation of being crazy, people didn't take the old man seriously, and they think he died after strangling himself on the twenty-two scapulars, because no one could explain what had happened when they found his body covered with feathers in a ditch.

She gets up first, before me and the wings, which don't sleep. We simply talk that way. They spend the night moving in a nervous flutter that scares the mosquitoes, so in every house and on the streets a whirlwind is raised like the one made by the fan the Company put in the cantina, an imported contraption, brilliant and revolving, to make us feel good, cool off the drunks, and blow away the smell of vomit, the two hundred and more nocturnal regurgitations of garbanzos and chicken soup that we throw up when we leave work. Always. The women are used to this by now. Because of the vigilance of the wings, not because of us men or my grandfather, who spent his last years (while the first pair was growing) trampled on a sidewalk with a fortuneteller's sadness on him, a long-haired, distant wizard, slobbering over the pavement from a world before the metal case, pretending to wait for the sunrise (he didn't sleep), so that he could pick up his harangues again, dragging the many things that hung from his neck and his shoulders, and his ankles, and whether it was Monday or Tuesday or Sunday, he pulled himself together and continued, after a strange spinning that no one understood, the endless marauding in which he spoke of zebras, miscarriages, scorpions, and lying sorcerers.

The Company brought a lot of foreigners who talked to each other in another language. Grandfather wanted to meet them; being an incredulous and incorrigible old man, he was so suspicious that he learned that strange tongue, then doubted even more, he spied on them, got a purple scapular that he hurled in their faces every time he ran into them, and developed a sense of smell so extraordinary that he could smell them from a distance. He wrote sixty-eight prophecies on the walls of the temple where those from the Company prayed. Today the dust (he also spoke about this) has peacefully erased them with the smooth topping that falls like fine flour over the town. The day he died Grandfather sprinkled thirty buckets of urine that he had hidden for weeks at the entrance to the Company, delivered an extensive discourse in that other language, and later shit right in the very spot.

In the morning the plates and pitchers and all the dishes are covered with dust. The women finish cleaning and removing the dust (with special shovels the Company sells us) at eleven. That's why we don't eat breakfast. They take care of the children first, the smallest who still don't know it's necessary to sleep face down and who sometimes asphyxiate or wake up with stomachs filled with dust and have to be given an enema. You can't expect them to cover their faces with a sheet or learn not to touch the wings. We eat lunch in a hurry (the Company gives us ten minutes), and we try to cover the plate with something between bites on the days when the wings are hysterical and the dust is everywhere. Since the men with the red pointed hats have arrived, siesta has been done away with. We have one meal a day. In the afternoon, the women go on working the dust and making sure the children don't tease the wings. After lunch, when the children are outside, it's easier. The wings never leave the bedrooms. They stay there, flying, mute and blind, so white, powerful and slow, barely able to stay in the air. The shovels are wide and light and they look like huge spoons, but they don't last long. Every three months a man with a red pointed hat arrives and gives us a new one. It is included in the lists under the heading they call household expenses, where they deduct from salaries the veils our women use, the masks for children over five, the oil for the enemas, six containers to keep food in, and the cost of transporting the wings on Fridays and their concentrate. If there haven't been any victims or irreverent behavior, the Company gives us a bonus at the end of the year.

The pair of wings in my grandfather's time, the one that arrived pregnant, mother of all those now in existence, lives in the Company. It's never left. After the day it was shown briefly in the plaza, not a single person has seen it again. For a long time, no one spoke more about the pair of wings either, because the men with the red pointed hats kept the news of the thirty eggs it was carrying a secret. After two years, the first brood was born and in a few months several families had wings in their homes, still quiet and tender, but strong enough and determined to stay without the least intention of fleeing, near the ceiling and over the bed, moving with a distant and serene patience so that our forebears didn't have any presentiment of the future strength of the winds and dust that would be raised, like small whirlwinds around those houses, those closest to the Company, those that had been covered with dust first. People who found out immediately arrived at those houses and spent hours astonished, looking at the little pairs of wings, and their enthusiasm was so great and their commentaries so many that women stood in line, not wanting to miss the opportunity to admire them. They waited with eager, happy eyes and a few sprigs of flowers and many gifts. They also waited for some weeks at the entrance to the Company, which never opened, to take baskets of corn and oats, and holy water to the mother wing, but those women and the ones who came after died and were buried in the sepulchers of feathers in the cellar of the Company. That is where the dead will end up. They left their baskets and their hopes on the sidewalk, never thinking that my grandfather had robbed them, and they lived with the satisfaction of having contributed to the brood hens that followed the mother of the white creatures, paying no attention to the shouts of my grandfather who tried to break up that pilgrimage of charity and sacrifice with declarations that the mother was immortal, that it would permit no one to know its powers and its size, that it would go on laying eggs for hundreds of centuries and that someday the wings would darken the light of the sun.

Roberta's son, on a night of childish and adventurous insomnia, animated by illusions and dreams, tried to catch a wing to his right, to pet it, touch it, and play with that con-

stant splendor that flew near him and his parents. He had no
sooner finished jumping from the mattress to reach it when
one of the wings, as strong as the kick of a mule, flattened his
nose, knocked out some teeth and one eye, pushed in his forehead, pulled out his eyebrows, and left him mute for the rest
of his life. Roberta's son was one of those in charge of sweep-
ing the Company rooms. Those who perform this service are
deformed and mute, men (women don't work there) missing
an arm or a leg, who've lost half of their ribs or are missing
a lung. Others are stooped or pale or suffer from magma, a
contagious disease spread by the wings that scratches the face
and makes it break out in blisters and skin ulcers. The skin
loosens and falls and turns into a thin hide that sticks to the
bones and is blue. Others have no ears or are prematurely
bald. The common characteristic of the sweepers is that not
one of them speaks. An unexpected and mysterious event in
the Company has left them without tongues. Anibal, great
grandson of my grandfather, the centenarian, died from
being hit by a wing in the kidneys when he tried to change a
lightbulb (the Company brought in electric lights). He care-
lessly got too close to the wings, and since they float at a short
distance from the bed, they got him in the back and broke his
spine. In the morning they offered the official condolences
and buried him in feathers. Uriel, the son of the only woman
who believed my grandfather (which is why he hung himself)
wanted to puncture the side of the wings with a penknife one
heedless and mad dawn that cost him his life, because before
he could deliver his blow, his skull was already smashed to
bits. Severiano—a hapless disciple of the fortuneteller, who
accompanied him in his defiance, left him alone, and was his
gutter friend, getting him out of jams, a youth who respected
him in a dignified, measured way, who got him on his feet

and gave him a cane—died of being hit by a wing when he jumped the adobe wall and entered the Company yard.

Tomorrow is Friday. They will take away the wings. At six the town will be in darkness. The Company turns off the lights, so we grope our way between the two rooms (in the houses they gave us there are only two rooms and one bed; the men with the red pointed hats say that families should sleep in the same bed). Since candles or matches aren't allowed that night and they make us keep absolutely silent until five in the afternoon on Saturday, we don't do anything but sit and watch the dark and feel the silky eternal white dust brush over our bodies. Anyway, the dust is part of our lives, something we possess, like the wings, which gives sense to our antlike activity, to the ten hours a day that we work, moving it from one place to another, over here, over there, piling it up in twenty-meter-high hills on Mondays. Tuesdays we undo these hills and sweep uniformly toward the west, and Wednesdays we form little mounds in front of every door. Thursdays we toss the little mountains upward as high as we can. Fridays we gather up the dust and lay it down in lines along the length of the streets. Saturdays we wet it down with Company hoses, and Sundays we make mudballs that dry and disintegrate at four o'clock. Mondays we go back to making hills.

Translated by Barbara Ras

We Have Brought You the Sea

Uriel Quesada

FOR TEN YEARS, I haven't been to the sea. I want to see it so badly that this morning I begged my mother until I made her break down in tears. I remember the sea, despite how long it's been and how small I was then. I can almost make out its rhythmic motion, its sound, as if it were chewing sand, its far boats in their rise and fall over the rumps of waves.

I was six years old back then. It was the first time I saw the sea, and Papa promised me we'd return other summers, but he never kept his promise. Later came the pains, the headaches, the day in October when for the first time I couldn't hold myself up. These long boring years in bed, inventing and believing promises that—like going back to the beach— would never come true. One by one I remember the most important ones: first, to make me well; later, a teacher so I could finish my studies; the wheelchair so I could leave the house; the easy chair so I wouldn't always have to be in bed, the books with big pictures, the portable radio. Soon they'll offer to bring me a priest so I can make peace with God, but I know they won't bring him. For me—someone with so much time, removed from the world for so long, a prisoner guilty of nothing, with no chance of escaping from an old room—what could I do to hurt or damage anyone?

Still, I shouldn't be ungrateful. As poor as they are, they've given me something, sacrificing to support my sickness. Since they were convinced of the inefficiency of the Social Security Hospital, and hoping the diagnosis was wrong, they paid a neurologist for a couple of private consultations. I heard the doctor tell them the only thing to do was to wait and ask the Lord for a miracle. When the doctor said good-bye, saying he would not return, I breathed easier, since now they wouldn't have to admit to not having enough money to continue the treatment.

They've also bought some stuff I didn't have any use for. Some dark glasses, a basketball, a couple of cans of peaches, and a nougat imported from Spain. On the other hand, I accepted a Bible from them and let them take me to Easter week ceremonies and make a promise to the Virgin. The saints didn't hear us; neither did God. My family got even poorer, and everyone gave up a lot of things to gladden my slow agony.

Sophie and Lalo work. Cuyo wants to quit school to follow them. Papa drinks a lot more now, and at times I've heard him say it's because of me. Now Mama doesn't need to cry as much as before. Her eyes are sunken in, and even her smiles reveal a bitter impatience and resignation. Maybe it's the only thing that God has granted us.

I don't read the Bible anymore, not even the part about Lazarus or the blind man or the one possessed. I just want to die. I know I'm going to die. They haven't told me, but I know. You can feel it in the house, see it in their gestures, hear it in their sighs. I've been suffering for so long that I'm already used to the pain. I don't need the pills or the syrups. It's been months since I've taken them. I throw the remedies into the cracks of the floor so they think I'm following the treatment. I don't deceive myself. What I want is to die. I smile. I don't complain. I please them with my pious enthusiasm, but now not one hope is left. I'm certain only of dying, and I wish for it soon, today, right now.

As a last wish, I would love to see the sea. In my dreams, that longing filled me, that impossibility, that joke, because anyone, except me, could get to the sea in two hours. Like an impulse to break out of the enclosure of all these years. I begged Mama to take me until we both parted in tears. "How would we get there?" "Who would be up to the adventure of transporting a person at death's door from here to the coast?" Where would they get the money to take me? If it took them a month to buy the peaches and they had to deprive Cuyo of the blanket he needed so badly?

By noon Mama hadn't stopped sobbing. She didn't tidy up the house or make lunch. My aunt and uncle arrived with Papa and my cousins. On the other side of the wall I could hear them talking among themselves before the oldest came in to try to change my mind, to tell me to ask for something else. It's not just a question of *colones*, Papa said. You wouldn't be able to manage such a tiring trip.

I insisted until I thought I had moved them. They went to look for a car and everyone chipped in some money. But by the time the stupor of one o'clock arrived, there wasn't the slightest chance of a trip. Before I fell asleep, my little cousins came up to me to ask if I really wanted to see the sea. I answered drowsily that it was all I yearned for.

I'm awake again. Mama has come into the room. Her face is pale, dark lines under her eyes. She's trembling. I've lived long enough to hear my mother say an emphatic no. There's no automobile; there's no money; no, she can't go on the train; no, there won't be a trip today, but maybe tomorrow . . .

"And if tomorrow is too late?"

Mama has gone to cry again in the living room, and the house is empty because my aunt and uncle don't want to be saddened by her weeping.

I want to see the sea, I repeat, shouting, I want to see the sea.

Then my little cousins come in again. One stays at the door, keeping watch. Another opens the window and with the girls, he drags the cot so that I can see the blue sky, uncovers me so I can feel the breeze coming in. The others have taken a sheet, holding it tense to produce a rhythmic sound all the cousins recognize. I feel the taste of salt water in my mouth, while the children imitate sounds of seagulls or the whistles of boats. Later, the youngest girl comes up to me with a conch shell that I enclose in my hands, and a snail shell I put next to my ear. For everyone, she says: "Look! We have brought you the sea. If you want to see it, now all you have to do is close your eyes."

Translated by Barbara Ras

Mint Flowers

Alfredo Aguilar

I REMEMBER THAT MANUELA DIED before midnight, the same day she saw the mint bloom in her patio. The day she told us she would die. It was April, a fine month to be born, not to die.

As soon as she came upon the fragrant white clusters of mint flowers, time was short and she had many affairs to settle before dying. The first thing she did was find the priest to hear her confession and give her absolution; then she turned to putting her earthly affairs in order. On her way home she went by the *pulpería* and paid the week's bill, she chatted with Julio, the owner, and said good-bye to his wife, gave the children her blessing, and continued up the street, taking in every detail of everything in sight. The coffee plantations were beginning to bloom and the song of the *yigüirros* announced that winter was near. With a certain nostalgia she thought of summer, the sun shining above the hills and burning the pastures, the cool morning breezes stripping the trees, the orange afternoons, and the dusty streets. What a shame to leave all this behind, summers with their blue skies and swarms of cicadas greeting the morning sun. She traveled further into winter and filled her lungs with that delicious fragrance the earth gives off with the first touch of rain. Surely everything on earth, no matter how ugly, has its beautiful side, even winter with its morning cold that cuts us to our bones, with rain that falls like clockwork and dies drop by drop on the rooftops, lulling us to sleep, and those sad, gray dawns, little children running to school, splashing in puddles, looking up so the rain might fall in their faces—it was such a funny feeling that made us close our eyes even when we knew nothing would happen to us, and yet as we tried to open them, our instinct to keep them shut was so much stronger.

It's sad to leave all this behind, but never mind, everything comes to an end after all, there's nothing left but to accept my death just like my grandfather did that morning he was walking to the orchard carrying a couple of gophers and he came upon the scent of thick clusters of white mint flowers in his patio and then it was my father's turn; the poor men didn't even have a chance to confess, because in those days we didn't have a priest in town and going to La Villa was nearly impossible. At least I had that advantage.

At that time of day the town looked deserted, everyone was busy with their daily chores: men in the coffee plantations and women at home, putting up with annoying children, and it's already ten and I haven't even made lunch and my husband's back at twelve.

As she walked along the plaza, Manuela saw a dust devil taking shape in one corner, raising dust, dry leaves, and garbage; it moved quickly and aimlessly, as birds do when they're learning to fly and don't know where to go. The same thing happened to the dust devil, its inexperience took it crashing against Tito's bar, and he came out complaining about the

garbage it had left behind. Manuela stood there watching.
Tito greeted her amiably and she told him that you shouldn't
get so angry, thank God you've got all the time in the world
to watch dust devils come and go, and Tito answering her,
you will see them for a long time too, and Manuela answered
him that no, she wouldn't, I'm dying tonight, what? that's
right, didn't you know that I saw the mint bloom today, and
she continued on her way. For a few minutes Tito stood at the
door to his shop, looking like someone who has seen death
walk by and can't grasp the full extent of what's happening,
and yet he still manages to wave good-bye to her. Manuela
disappeared amid the cloud raised by a new dust devil, this
one in the middle of the street.

I don't mean to be ungrateful, but I would have liked living
a bit longer, I would have liked knowing some places other
than this damned town, even though now that I think about
it, it must be more difficult to accept death when you've come
to know more, when you have a lot to leave behind. My God,
what am I thinking? I'm sorry, I didn't mean to offend you,
it's not that I haven't accepted your decision, just that I think
it would be better if we knew at birth the day we would die.
Then maybe what's happening to me right now wouldn't
happen; my eyes hurt as I strain to see everything I can; I'm
hardly blinking as I try not to squander any more time; we
wouldn't waste a single minute with so much nonsense and
gossip and getting into things that are none of our business.

Jumping from one thought to another she arrived home
and found Dora, her daughter, hurriedly grinding corn and
cleaning the house—a funeral always demands a lot of extra
work. Manuela didn't pay much attention to her daughter's
bustling, since she had to get ready for her own funeral.

What she did take care of personally was her shroud; she

took the habit of the Virgen del Carmen from the dresser and ironed it. As she did so she felt her head being invaded by images, feelings, memories, all of them a total disorder, and she had no time because none of them would last long enough for her to identify. My God, what's happening to me? Is this what happens to everyone who's about to die? I'm sure it is. The worst thing is not knowing where one's going, not that I doubt Heaven's existence, no, not at all, what terrifies me is not knowing what Heaven's like, and, worse yet, they could send me to Hell. I wonder what Hell's like? Or Purgatory? No doubt my first stop will be Purgatory, everyone who dies goes through there. Who knows how long they'll leave me there, hopefully not long. It's so hard to live life without sinning and to say good-bye to your life, even when it hasn't given you much to begin with, and it's already three in the afternoon. What have I done during these last hours? It seems like I just got back, maybe the clock's running fast again, no, it can't be, Alejandro's up and he gets up at about three. Well, I'm running out of time. I guess it's true that nobody dies ahead of schedule. Who would have thought yesterday that I'd die today? If anybody had told me, I certainly wouldn't have believed it, feeling as healthy as I have recently, even that dry cough that's been bothering me has gone away. Hard to believe, but it took me seventy years to realize that in the end my life's been an interminable chain of large and small failures, a race against time, thousands of sacrifices, constant self-denial, miracles that never happened, and what's left the day you die? Nothing. More than thirty years of putting up with a husband who filled me with little ones—I had eight of them but only four survived and the others went the way of diarrhea and worms, and of those that survived only Dora will make it, she's the only one who was born with all her wits about her, the other three together don't add up to one, they never got beyond first grade and that's it, they don't work, never bathe, when they can they get drunk, and now that I'm leaving, who's going to take care of them? Probably nobody, but that's life, they'll just have to get along somehow. Strange things happen to you, like the four little children that died on us, I've never been able to forget them, and that's counting the fact that not one of them made it past three. I still remember their innocent faces looking amazed at what was happening, as if protesting that we should let them die without taking them to the doctor, there wasn't any money and La Villa was so far away, and I'd spend day after day and night after night watching over their sleep, trying to bring down their fevers with cold washcloths and giving them teas to drink of mallow, of *yantén,* of chamomile, which wouldn't do a thing, and look here, Toño, this little one's going to die, and Toño, What do you want me to do? Can't you see I barely make enough to eat? Then we should think about not having any more children, this is a sin, Manuela, what are you saying? Slowly but surely, Toño's face appeared from the dark corners of her memory, as if it had come from a deep sleep, until finally she saw it clearly before her, and along with him the memory of those interminable nights of imposed love, repressed and gagged, his shining eyes, his rapid breath and his caresses, as he got closer to me, and not now, Toño, the children aren't asleep and they'll notice, don't be an idiot, woman, they're too little and they don't understand, and I'm already up against the wall, and Toño has her pinned on all four sides and his breath burns my face and then she lets him do what he wants to because a woman shouldn't deny her husband even if she thinks it's a sin to be bringing children into the world to die before they're five.

The following month once again the nausea, the vomiting, and worst of all the terrible anxiety and fear of having to tell Toño that I'm pregnant again, because as usual he's going to be furious and tell me it's all my fault, and she'd end up crying because after all she wasn't the only one responsible for the children. I lived thirty-odd years with him before he died, making love every other day, and she remembered that she enjoyed only the first year of her marriage, after that she was more worried about getting pregnant, I couldn't concentrate and once I'd overcome my fear, Toño was already done and would turn over. Even the memory of those nights continues to torture me, and she decided not to think about him anymore, because I want to leave this world with my share of bitterness untouched.

By five in the afternoon Manuela had settled her business and she took to giving away her few belongings to her closest friends and relatives. An old alarm clock with two bells that could wake up the dead was for her son Ramón, let's see if maybe you'll wake up early; a little box in which she kept buttons of different colors and shapes, spools of thread, pins, needles, a thimble, and all kinds of trinkets, she gave to Dora. Then she took her greatest treasures: the multicolored prints of saints and her medals of San Gerardo, San Felipe, and the rest of the celestial court, and she began dividing them up among her grandchildren, and as for me, since I was such a good friend of the family, I received a print of San Judas and a medal of San Cristóbal, just in case you get a car someday, then he'll keep you from getting into an accident.

Once everything was divided up, the only thing left to do was get dressed. She put on the habit of the Virgen del Carmen, she hung a scapular around her neck, combed what hair she had into a bun, and lay down. By that time the whole town knew Manuela was going to die that very night, but few of us were lucky enough to see her alive before she closed herself in her bedroom and advised us not to open the door before midnight, at which time her daughter decided to go in and found her on the bed, with a rosary in her hands, her index fingers and thumbs holding the beads on the fifth Lord's Prayer of the third mystery, her eyes closed and her mouth tightly shut, perhaps holding back the kind of pain you feel when something inside gives up. Dora walked up to her and in the semi-darkness she put her hand on her chest, on the left side, right where the heart is, and confirmed that she was dead. She came out, announced the news, and the pious old women in town began their lamentations and their prayers.

An hour later, Rafa, Dora's husband, arrived with the coffin, and Manuela was placed in it and moved to the parlor, where we lined up to see her face through a glass plate that steamed up as people walked past, until she couldn't be seen anymore. Then they decided to remove the cover completely so they could close it the following day before the burial. That's what gave us the chance to place among her fingers, which were yellowed from tobacco smoke, an enormous branch of aromatic white flowers we cut from the mint in her patio, the same mint that had told Manuela she would die before midnight that very same day.

The next day in the afternoon, when the sun's rays were less intense, we buried her. Nobody left without first throwing a handful of dirt into the grave, and when the sun hid and the sky began to darken, we left her alone, terribly alone among so many dead.

When we returned to her house to recite the first rosary of her novena, we found that the mint blossoms in the patio had withered and that their fragrance had vanished; they were suddenly gone, as they had come, as life comes and goes.

Then we decided to go out and look for as much mint as we could find in the town and we pulled it up by the roots, and we burned it, destroyed it, but all our efforts were useless, since within days it sprouted back even more vigorously.

Many years passed and nobody saw it bloom, some people even came to think that what had happened to Manuela, her grandfather, and her father had been nothing more than a fatal coincidence. Until this morning when we stepped out into the street and found ourselves in air rarefied by the especially delicious fragrance of mint blossoms, and we realized that they had flowered again in Manuela's patio and that Dora, her daughter, had found them that morning when she was out gathering firewood.

Tabito, her son, came looking for me to tell me what had happened and to ask me to go with them, with him and his father, to the cemetery, it was time to move Manuela's bones, they'd need her niche by tomorrow afternoon. When we uncovered the vault we found the box completely undone and Manuela's bones made smooth by the work of worms. We pulled out the board on which she was resting, and we could see the entire skeleton, like the one we had in school for anatomy class. We found a rosary with black beads among her ribs, her hands were still held together, and there, intact, was the branch of white mint blossoms we had placed on her breast the day of the vigil, still fresh, dampened by dew, casting its intoxicating fragrance that is now beginning to flood the cemetery.

Translated by Mathew Quilter

When New Flowers Bloomed

Carmen Naranjo

IT WAS AND STILL IS a round town that makes a circle in the hollow. The houses face the mountains, and seeing them you can predict the weather: it will be hot; it will rain; the wind tonight will be terrible; a calm day, perhaps sultry, around four o'clock the rain will start to fall; it will dawn drizzling; there may be a tremor today.

A town that grew and shrank according to the unsteadiness of the country; sometimes the town leaders would think about agriculture, at others about industry, always about commerce, most of them about seeing that everything went along as it should, calmly, without worsening the poverty of so many poor. A town with eucalyptus, orange trees, cypresses, *manzanas de agua*, dusty streets, orchards, chayote fields, happy shouts from everyone meeting and greeting one another with joy, chattiness, toads, *yigüirros*, and a sky convulsed with clouds. The houses were built with whatever was at hand—wood, bricks, zinc, inclement weather, wind, cold, heat, some decorated flowerpots and primitive unkempt gardens where the chickens wandered among the marigolds and the ducks among the lilies.

A tranquil town in which an old man dies between the recounting of his death throes and the inventory of what he left: a yoke from the beginning of the century, an abandoned mortar, a strange sewing machine for sewing who-knows-what, some open-toed shoes, a completely rusted shaving razor. A peaceful town in which the birth of a child is shouted from hallway to hallway, alley to alley. It was a girl. Another one. Poor things, what are they going to do with so many? And illness, combatted with medicine prescribed by the doctor and with herbs recommended by those who know about those things.

A town that always faces toward the mountain and admires, loves, and respects it; please, God, don't let it come down on top of us, because then we wouldn't even be able to tell what happened. And the mountain, always changing, brings them news of events that their timid, shut-in minds don't dare consider. A new priest will arrive—don't take him too seriously—he's obsessed with sin, poor sinner, everything frightens him, don't be frightened. And in the summer two young and ingenuous young people will come; you'll never have such an incredible opportunity to depend on such excellent teachers. They'll teach you what had been forgotten a long time ago and what it's necessary to remember so that new flowers can bloom.

It was a time when the town almost became a village. The young people emigrated in search of work and a different life. The ravine smothered them and the slimness of the mountain. Some had stayed: the old ones, old grandparents and great-grandparents, a couple of great-great-grandmothers totally committed to God, and the parents prematurely aged and disconnected by the accelerated change brought on by the telegraph, the telephone, radio, and television.

She arrived first, one Sunday on the last of the four buses; she was going to take care of the school and teach first through sixth grades to the reduced population of school-age kids, nearly thirty children, ages seven to twelve. Her name preceded her. Eugenia María de los Angeles Rivera Mancilla, born in a place known as the Cumbres de lo Alto for the Perfection of the Holy Birth. She looked very pale, too young for that rabble of sparrow-hawks, but the mountain told them that she was the one, the one expected, the one who dominates the winds and knows her letters, and that behind those blue eyes resides the wisdom of life.

Eugenia María de los Angeles stopped on a corner and ran her eyes over the row of houses that required only a few seconds of investigation to reveal that she was at the ends of the earth. She raised her eyes to the majesty of the mountain to verify rapidly that she was at the beginning of manifestly beautiful things, which she knew were not given gratuitously or by chance but for legitimate merit, earned through will and that stubborn tenacity for overcoming adversity.

Her first lesson was brilliant. She kept the kids awake, despite the fact that they'd gotten up before the mountain could become a profile, a black and threatening shadow, rather less like a grid of unruly trees and weeds in the disorder of God, who was quite disorganized when it came to the spontaneous growth of nature. She simply showed maps and contrived to stimulate curiosity about the flat vision of the everyday.

The announced priest didn't arrive, because the decision to transfer Father Toño had been changed. With a certain inertia he had been doing good work; at least he hadn't provoked any complaints or unnecessary intrigues or problems with the ever-tranquil, patient community.

The young man arrived eight days later, carrying his youth

on his back and his enthusiasm for beginning his first professional job in the administration of a farm that had everything and was going to cultivate even more.

They met in front of the school with burning glances. He couldn't help himself and approached, holding out his open hand. José Luis Villacencio, at your service. She smiled in the most natural way imaginable, an inextinguishable, inexhaustible smile.

From then on, during their free time, they were inseparable; they went to the plaza, they walked tirelessly down all the paths of the town. For them the birds sang, the flowers opened, the eucalyptus perfumed the air, day and night began, clouds turned a chalky white, twilights lengthened.

No one in the town said a word; it seemed very natural to them, they were so perfectly matched, so close.

One day the little old lady Refugio, one of the oldest of the village, watched them for a long time. But what was this? That way of slowly passing his finger down her arm, from her shoulder to her fingertip, tirelessly. Then that touching of heads, and how they petted each other, just like puppies. She associated the scene with an old rosebush that had begun to bloom with true passion, after years and years of dormancy. Something strange is happening, she thought; her blood circulated faster and her rheumatism pains had vanished. Later from watching so much, she made others watch as well, and she saw they were excited, enthused, absorbed by that torrent of true caresses.

That night the old woman didn't sleep; the hours passed as she remembered their exact movements and searched in vain for happiness. The following morning she had made up her mind, and at dusk she passed again through the plaza, and the whole town was there watching and watching. She saw what she could as long as it was light, and then went down river looking for don Miguel, who was almost as old as she was. That night she slept like a log.

The couple became the number one spectacle of the town; now no one read, not even the newspaper; in the *pulpería* the television stopped glowing; in the houses the radios were turned off; no one was interested in the soccer game; not even the players wanted to wear themselves out with running and kicking. The priest and the sexton, together with the altar boys, joined the watching. It was a lovely spectacle, so pure and innocent that the priest dedicated Sunday's sermon to the art of loving, loving each other endlessly, without respite.

Strange things began to happen in the town. The potatoes tasted like yams, the yams like papaya, the papaya like turnips, the turnips like tomatoes, the coffee bean while it was still green smelled like orange blossoms, daisies bloomed from rose bushes, gladiolus from tulips, and bougainvillea from lilies. Everyone realized that summer was staying around too long and it wasn't raining; there wasn't even a hint of rain in the sky, only chalky white clouds. But they didn't worry, because the river brought more water than ever and it was as soothing as the sea; it caressed them to sleep with caresses that were more creative, more imaginative by the day, as the river slowly carried out its journey.

When the old woman admitted she was pregnant, they thought it was her senility or maybe nostalgia for other times; she had given birth to nine children, she had almost sixty-five grandchildren, and her eighth great-grandchild was about to be born. They started believing it when it appeared that all the women, old ones and young ones, some of them mere girls, were in the same state, along with the sacristan's wife, the girlfriends of the altar boys, and the priest's blessed servant.

The scent of flowers truly intoxicated the village; they bloomed everywhere, even among the stones; the plaza was filled with them, and the paths, and the sidewalks, to the point that it was hard to walk and to find a place to stop, calmly without feeling guilty for hurting some abundant plant.

Perhaps that was why people stopped going out and didn't realize that the couple wasn't there anymore. They had gone, each their separate way, as they had arrived, each one on different days.

He left first. In that town, filled with flowers, of tranquil good people and a smiling priest who always put good before evil, he realized that he had made a mistake in his calling. He wanted to be a sailor, not a farmer. She left afterward, perhaps a few weeks later. By then her smile had dissipated and her eyes filled with solitude, the solitude of an island in an unruly sea where someone was shipwrecked.

Neither of them perceived anything different in that town, so quiet and so covered with flowers. She left as if shutting a door, he as if opening one.

When the town realized they had gone, busy as everyone was with babies being born (almost all around the same date) and with the care of that enormous number of children—there were many twins and triplets—another teacher was already there who had arrived obviously pregnant, and another farm administrator, with his wife and five rather grown children.

Now it rained day and night, the flowers had disappeared, the river ran with less music and less water, things tasted like what they were, plants produced what they were supposed to. Everyone confessed his derangement to the priest, and the priest sought out his superior to do the same. He took comfort in the fact that his superior told him solemnly what he himself had repeated in the confessional: one swallow doesn't a summer make, nor does the song of the *yigüirro* bring the rains. The ephemeral has no transcendence, and if the derangement had been arranged, it didn't have the gravity of a sin.

The couple appeared in some dreams but without doing much damage; everyone had rediscovered that you sleep better and more profoundly in the solitude of yourself and acting your age.

Translated by Linda Britt

Glossary

bobo: A vegetarian fish prized for its meat. A member of the mullet family, it inhabits the rapids of rivers in the Atlantic Zone, often weighing up to thirty pounds.

burrocar: a railroad cart pulled along the rails by mules.

calalú: a plant eaten for both its tender leaves and tubers.

carbonero: someone who makes or sells charcoal.

chiainarrú: a tuber used to make a soft drink.

chumico tree (Curatella americana): a tree with large rough leaves used for polishing or finishing wood. The round black seeds, chumicos, are used by children for marbles.

colon(es): Costa Rica's monetary unit.

curandero: someone who heals with folk remedies.

curraré: a variety of plantain noted for its enormous size.

finca: farm.

gallo pinto: a fried mixture of rice and black beans commonly eaten for breakfast.

garrobo (Basiliscus basiliscus): the basilisk, a large lizard shaped like an iguana, with crests on its head, back, and tail. Popularly called the Jesus Christ lizard for its ability to run across streams and ponds on its hind legs. Garrobo also refers to the ctenosaur (*Ctenosaura similis*), a large iguanid lizard widely hunted for its edible flesh, which is reputed to be a cure for impotence.

guanábana (Annona muricata): soursop; a dark green tropical fruit up to a foot long; oval-shaped and covered with long, curved, fleshy spinules. Its white flesh is often used for juice drinks.

guabina: name generally applied to a large member of the goby family (Gobiidae), marine fish that also live in rivers and brackish water. Commonly spelled *guavina*.

guarumo: any of the common trees in Costa Rica belonging to *Cecropia*. Its leaves resemble fig leaves, and its hollow, whitish trunks are often inhabited by ants. Because of its sprawling, candelabra-shaped branches, the guarumo is one of the few trees in which sloths can be readily seen.

guineos: small plantains.

hoja de aire (Kalanchoe pinnata): commonly called air plant, Mexican love plant, and miracle plant. The leaves have the ability to grow after being separated from the plant, even out of water or soil.

jaquí: a tree that produces a delicious red fruit.

jejenes: sand fleas; no-see-ums.

machaca: a silvery freshwater fish; adults range from five to twenty pounds. Principally vegetarian, they can be found below the overhanging branches of fruit trees growing on riverbanks, waiting to eat fruit that drops into the river.

machetero: one who works with a machete. In Costa Rica, as in much of Latin America, the long, wide-bladed knife is put to an astonishing range of uses, from clearing jungle to cutting lawns.

manzana de agua: mountain apple; a white oval fruit that resembles an apple in texture.

Meseta Central: Central Basin; used to describe the highland valley around San José.

monjarra: usually spelled *mojarra*. Name generally applied to small cichlids, a group of perch-like tropical fish diverse and abundant in Central America.

mozote: an herb popularly used to cure hangovers.

muchacho(s): boy(s).

nance (Byrsonima crassifolia): shoemaker's tree; a small tree that produces a round yellow edible fruit (some species sweet, others bitter) that is sold in markets and by street vendors.

OIJ: Organization of Judicial Investigation—the police arm of the Supreme Court.

oropéndola (Zarhynchus wagleri): a bird common to the Caribbean lowlands and other low areas of Costa Rica; a member of the family that contains American orioles and grackles. Its nests are large pouches (up to 6 feet long), woven out of vines and plant fibers and attached to the ends of branches, where they are plainly visible dangling in groups against the sky.

palmitero: a harvester of hearts of palm, the soft palm tissue eaten as a delicacy.

patrón/patrona: boss.

pejibaye: the orange to reddish fruit of the pejibaye palm. Eaten cooked, sometimes with mayonnaise, it has a dry, starchy consistency and a chestnut-like taste. Though it grows in much of tropical America, the fruit is popularly eaten only in Costa Rica; commonly sold by street vendors, whose carts, equipped with pots for cooking the fruit, brighten the streets with colorful arrays of shiny pejibayes.

pejibaye palm (Bactris gasipaes): peach palm; a tree with a spiny trunk that grows to 15 meters in height. Occurs naturally as well as in cultivated groves. It produces clusters of fruit and is the source of hearts of palm. Male flowers drop off the tree within twenty-four hours of blossoming, sometimes falling all at once to produce a "rain of flowers" (J. Beech in *Costa Rican Natural History,* p. 100).

pesos: the monetary unit of several Spanish-speaking countries; used generically in Costa Rica to refer to money (*colones*).

pizote (Nasua narica): white-nosed coati; a small diurnal mammal related to the raccoon. It has a long snout and a long, slender tail.

plátano: plantain; a large banana, cooked both green and ripe in a variety of ways. A staple food in the tropics.

Pocomía: voodoo.

provinciano: a person from the provinces.

pulpería: a "corner" store; occasionally refers to a place that sells drinks as well as staples. In Costa Rica the word is used in place of the "tienda" of other Latin American countries.

rancho: hut; home.

reina de la noche: a shrub common to river valleys, whose leaves are used as a folk remedy for curing facial inflammations. Its large white bell-shaped flowers give off a strong perfume at night.

róbalo: snook; a carniverous ocean fish that also moves into river estuaries; belongs to the genus *Centropomus*. It is the center of the economy for villages on the northern Atlantic coast.

roncador: ocean fish of the grunt family that occasionally enters rivers; belongs to the family *Pomadasyidae*. The name comes from the audible sound the fish makes by grinding together its pharyngeal teeth.

targuá: a tree common to the environs of San José and other temperate regions of Costa Rica. Its leaves are large and round, and before falling they turn a distinctive reddish color. The trunk releases a gummy substance when cut, which is reputed to make an excellent toothpaste.

tepemechín: another species of mullet of the genus *Agnosthomus*. Smaller than the *bobo*, it inhabits coastal drainages and estuaries and feeds on algae.

tepezcuintle: paca; a large nocturnal mammal distantly related to the guinea pig. It ranges through Central America and is hunted for its meat. A similar rodent, the agouti, or *guatusa*, is diurnal.

Tico/a(s): Costa Rican(s). The name comes from the Costa Ricans' custom of frequently using the diminutive in their speech, (e.g., "*momentico,*"), formed by adding the variant "*tico*" to the ends of words.

toboba: Bothrops asper; fer-de-lance; a large brown patterned
   snake with a triangular head, justly feared for its potent
   venom and its readiness to attack when approached. It grows
   up to six feet in length. The young are arboreal; mature
   snakes, terrestrial. Also called *terciopelo.*
yantén (Plantago major): a medicinal plant that grows in wet
   places; commonly used as a remedy for stomachaches.
yerbabuena: mint.
yigüirro (Turdus grayi): clay-colored robin, Costa Rica's national
   bird, whose song is said to call the rains of winter. In Costa
   Rica, where the year-round temperature varies little, winter
   refers to the wet months from May to November.
yocotó: a leafy plant used instead of lettuce in the tropics.
zompopa(s): leaf-cutting or "parasol" ants. They carry chunks of
   leaves in their jaws back to nests in the ground, where using a
   complex combination of leaf matter, saliva, and feces, the ants
   grow a fungus, which they harvest for food.

ABOUT THE EDITORS

BARBARA RAS is a prize-winning poet who has traveled widely in Central and South America. Her first book of poems, *Bite Every Sorrow* (LSU Press), won the Walt Whitman Award and the Kate Tufts Discovery Award. Her collection *One Hidden Stuff* (Penguin) was picked by the *San Antonio Express-News* as one of the ten best books of 2006. Ras's work has appeared in the *New Yorker, TriQuarterly, Gulf Coast, Orion, Massachusetts Review,* and others. She lives in San Antonio and directs Trinity University Press.

OSCAR ARIAS, former president of Costa Rica and recipient of the Nobel Peace Prize, is currently president of the Arias foundation.

ALFREDO AGUILAR (1959 –) has published a book of short stories and is currently at work on a novel. He won the Primer Certamen de Literatura Joven Centroamericana in 1988 for *Morir dos veces*, the collection from which the story included here was taken.

ALFONSO CHASE (1945–) was born in Cartago. He is a poet, essayist, and fiction writer. He has published eight books, including stories for children. Professor of literature at the Universided Nacional de Costa Rica, he edited a two-volume survey of Costa Rican fiction entitled *La narrative contemporanea de Costa Rica* (1975). His collection of short stories, *El hombre que se quedó adentro del sueño*, was published in 1994.

FABIÁN DOBLES (1918–1997) was a major voice in Costa Rican literature. His work expresses a vision of rural Costa Rican life, dramatizing the life and themes of the common people. He wrote fiction, poetry, and nonfiction and worked at an astonishing variety of professions, from milkman to editor to president of a Costa Rican-Soviet cultural exchange organization. He was honored by many prizes, including the Premio Nacional de Cultura Magón. Among his many books are *Los años, pequeños dias, Historias de Tata Mundo,* and *Ese que llaman pueblo*.

LOUIS DUCOUDRAY (1942–) is one of the founders of modern architecture in Costa Rica. In 1976 he won the Premio Nacional Aquileo J. Echeverría for his short story collection *Elagua secreto*. He lives in a beach town on the Atlantic Coast.

QUINCE DUNCAN (1940–) was born in San José of Jamaican ancestry and was raised in the banana-growing region of the Atlantic Coast. He has written nonfiction and fiction. His stories, set in the environs of Limón, explore the social milieu of Costa Rica's blacks. His works of fiction include *Final de calle* and *Kimbo*.

FERNANDO DURÁN AYANEGUI (1939–) is a native of Alajuela, the setting for his story included here. He studied chemistry in Cuba, where he received his doctorate. He was the rector of the Universidad de Costa Rica. He is the author of many works of fiction, including *Cuentos para Laura, Cuando desaparecieron los topos,* and *Opus 13 para cimarrona.*

CARLOS LUIS FALLAS (1909–1965) was known for his realism and for his championing of the proletariat. He worked on the United Fruit Company's banana plantations and was instrumental in organizing the workers there. He became active in politics and went on to serve as a deputy in the Costa Rican Congress. His works include *Mamita Yunai, Gentes y gentecillas,* and *Mi Madrina.* He won the Premio Nacional de Cultura Magón in 1965.

MARIO GONZÁLEZ FEO (1897–1969) was a reporter and columnist, and the author of books of chronicles and stories. His published books are *Nihil, Nihil II,* and *María de la soledad* (1967).

JOAQUÍN GUTIÉRREZ (1918–2000) wrote short stories, novels, poems, and journalism. Among his works of fiction are *Cocorí, Puerto Limón, Manglar,* and *Murámonos, Federico,* for which he won the Premio Nacional Aquileo J. Echeverría in 1973. For many years a dedicated leftist, he lived in the

United States and Chile, his second home, before returning to San José.

MAX JIMÉNEZ (1900–1947) spent much of his time abroad in Paris and other European and American cities. He painted in addition to writing poetry and fiction. His prose works include *Unos fantoches* and *El jaúl,* from which "The Palmitero" is excerpted.

CARMEN LYRA (1888–1949) was the pseudonym of María Isabel Carvajal. She left Costa Rica for political reasons and died in Mexico. Much beloved for her children's stories, she has also written to great acclaim for adults. Her most popular work is *Los cuentos de mi Tía Panchita* (1920).

CARMEN NARANJO (1931–) has been director of EDUCA (the publishing house for Central American universities), Minister of Culture, and ambassador to Israel. Her many books of poetry and fiction have received the highest honors. Her collection of stories *There Never Was a Once Upon a Time* is available in English, and her stories in translation lend their titles to the Central American anthologies *And We Sold the Rain* and *When New Flowers Bloomed.* Other work is included in *Short Stories by Latin American Women: The Magic and the Real* and *Women's Fiction from Latin America.*

YOLANDA OREAMUNO (1916–1956) began publishing as a student in the influential literary journal *Repertorio americano,* in which *"El espíritu de mi tierra"* first appeared. She traveled widely and spent part of her life in Mexico. Her work is collected in *A lo largo del corto camino* and *La ruta de su evasión.*

ABEL PACHECO (1933–) was raised in 24 Millas and Limón. He went on to study in San José and Mexico and later specialized in psychiatry in New Orleans and Europe. His works take place in a setting like the Zona Atlántica of his childhood, a world of two peoples—black and white—and their two cultures. He has published six books, among them *Paso de tropo, Una muchacha,* and *De la selva a la embajada.* He broadcasts a short daily television program called "Commentarios."

JULIETA PINTO (1922–) is the author of twelve books, most recently *Tierra de espejismos* (1991). Her books *La estación que sigue al verano* and *Los marginados* received the Premio Nacional Aquileo J. Echeverría. In English her work has been published in *When New Flowers Bloomed.*

URIEL QUESADA's first book is *Ese día de los temblores,* from which the story reproduced here is taken. In 1981 he won an essay contest for his work on Mario Vargas Llosa's *The Green House.*

SAMUEL ROVINSKI (1934–) has held various distinguished positions in the Costa Rican theatrical and literary worlds. He won the Premio Nacional Aquileo J. Echeverría for *La hora de los vencidos.* He has written essays, plays, and fiction. Among his works are *Ceremonia de casta, Las fisgonas de Paso Ancho,* and *El martirio del Pastor.* He has been anthologized in English in *Clamor of Innocence.*

CARLOS SALAZAR HERRERA (1906–1980) was an art professor at the Universidad de Costa Rica and the author of stories, poetry, and plays. His work has been widely translated into several languages. In 1964 he won Costa Rica's Premio Nacional de Cultura Magón.

Contributors

JOSÉ LEÓN SÁNCHEZ (1930–) was orphane
He spent twenty years in prison for attempte
Basilica de los Angeles in Cartago as part of
the Virgin's riches for indigenous people. W
prison at age nineteen he was illiterate. He has written ..
teen books, including *Tenochtitlán*, *La isla de los hombres solos*,
and *La cattleya negra*, and has many awards to his credit.

RIMA DE VALLBONA (1931–) is the author of twelve books
of short stories, novels, and essays. Among her published
works are *Mundo, demonio y mujer*, *Polvo del camino*, and *Cose-
cha de pescadores*. She has won several literary prizes both in
the United States and abroad, including Costa Rica's Premio
Nacional Aquileo J. Echeverría in 1968 for her novel *Noche
en vela*. She lives in Houston, Texas, where she teaches at
the University of Saint Thomas. Her work is anthologized in
English in *Clamor of Innocence*, *Beyond the Border: A New Age
in Latin American Women's Fiction*, and *Short Stories by Latin
American Women: The Magic and the Real*.

KIRK ANDERSON has translated Pedro Almodóvar's *Patty Diphusa and Other Writings* as well as works by José Luis Garci, Juan Miguel Asensi, Su Tong, and Zhong Ling, among others. He lives in Jamaica Plain, Massachusetts.

ZOE ANGLESEY's book of poems is entitled *Something More Than Force: Poems for Guatemala, 1971 – 1982*. She edited the bilingual *Ixok Amargo: Central American Women's Poetry for Peace* and *Stone on Stone*.

GABRIEL BERNS is Professor Emeritus of Spanish Literature, University of California at Santa Cruz. He has translated Rafael Alberti's autobiography, *The Lost Grove*, and has collaborated with the poet David Shapiro on a translation of Alberti's *Los 8 nombres de Picasso* (*The Eight Names of Picasso*).

LINDA BRITT is Assistant Professor of Spanish at the University of Maine at Farmington. She has published critical studies on Cervantes and García Lorca as well as on Carmen Naranjo.

PAMELA CARMELL has translated poems and prose by Gloria Fuertes, Belkis Cuza Malé, Antonio Larreta, Luis Arturo Ramos, and Soledad Puértolas. She is co-editor of an anthology of Spanish poets of the Generation of the 50s.

LELAND H. CHAMBERS's translations include *The Fear of Losing Eurydice* and *She Has Reddish Hair and Her Name Is Sabina*, both by Julieta Campos. He co-edited *To Tell the Tale:*

51 Short Stories by Central American Writers (1963 – 1988) and is widely published in various literary magazines.

CAROL CHRISTENSEN's translations include *Like Water for Chocolate*, by Laura Esquivel, and *The Harp and the Shadow*, by Alejo Carpentier. She lives in the San Francisco Bay Area.

JAMES HOGGARD, the author of twelve books and seven produced plays, teaches English at Midwestern State University in Wichita Falls, Texas. His translations, poems, stories, and essays have been widely published.

JOHN INCLEDON has translated, among other works, Salvador Elizondo's *Farabeuf* and *Day of the Winged Lion*, by Mario Luis Rodríguez. He teaches in the Department of Modern Languages and Literature at Albright College in Reading, Pennsylvania.

WILL KIRKLAND's translations include Rómulo Gallegos's classical Venezuelan novel about the rainforest, *Canaima*, and *The Gypsy Ballads*, by Federico García Lorca. His translations and original works are widely published in various literary journals. He lives in San Francisco.

ANGELA MCEWAN is a court interpreter, writer/translator, and Spanish teacher living in Whittier, California. She has worked as a bilingual editor for Doubleday Multimedia and for the National Multilingual Multicultural Materials Development Center. Her translations include the poems of Ana Rossetti.

MARY GOMEZ PARHAM, a Fulbright Scholar to Belize, edited a series of Belizean literary anthologies with her husband. She has published widely on topics in Latin American and Portuguese literature. She teaches Spanish at the University of Houston-Downtown.

BARBARA PASCHKE is a board member of the American Literary Translators Association (ALTA) and a freelance translator living in San Francisco. Her translations include *Riverbed of Memory*, poems by Daisy Zamora and short stories in two other Whereabouts Press books—*Cuba* and *Spain*. In addition, she has edited numerous other books and contributed to various journals.

MARGARET SAYERS PEDEN lives in Columbia, Missouri. Her translations include Pablo Neruda's *Selected Odes*, Isabel Allende's *The Infinite Plan*, Juan Rulfo's *Pedro Páramo*, and *An Ark for the Next Millennium*, a bestiary of poems by José Emilio Pacheco.

MATHEW QUILTER's translations include Carlos Castro Saavedra's *Adán Ceniza*, Giuseppe Pederiali's *Il drago nella fumana*, and Mario Benedetti's *Primavera con una esquina rota*. He lives in Berkeley, California.

MARK SCHAFER is a literary translator and teaches Spanish and Translation at the University of Massachusetts at Boston. He has translated *Cold Tales* and *René's Flesh* by Virgilio Piñera, and *Mogador* by Alberto Ruy Sánchez, among others.

"Mint Flowers" by Alfredo Aguilar was originally published in Spanish as "Las flores de las yerbabuenas" in *Morir dos veces* by EDUCA in San José, Costa Rica. © 1989 EDUCA. Translation © 1994 Mathew Quilter.

"Faust in Hatillo" by Alfonso Chase was originally published in Spanish as "Fausto en Hatillo" in *Ella usaba bikini* by Editorial Costa Rica in San José, Costa Rica. © 1991 Editorial Costa Rica. Translation © 1994 Leland H. Chambers.

"She Wore a Bikini" by Alfonso Chase was originally published in Spanish as "Ella usaba bikini" in *Ella usaba bikini* by Editorial Costa Rica in San José, Costa Rica. © 1991 Editorial Costa Rica. Translation © 1994 Leland H. Chambers.

"The Diary" by Fabián Dobles was originally published in Spanish as "El diario" in *La pesadilla y otros cuentos* by Editorial Costa Rica in San José Costa Rica. © 1984 Editorial Costa Rica. Translation © 1994 John Incledon.

"The Targuá Tree" by Fabián Dobles was originally published in Spanish as "El Targuá" in *La pesadilla y otros cuentos* by Editorial Costa Rica in San José, Costa Rica. © 1984 Editorial Costa Rica. Translation © 1994 John Incledon.

"Here" by Louis Ducoudray was originally published in Spanish as "Aquí" in *Narrativa contemporanea de Costa Rica*, ed. Alfonso Chase, by Ministry of Culture in San José, Costa Rica. © 1975 Alfonso Chase. Translation © 1994 Barbara Ras.

"The Oropéndolas" by Quince Duncan was originally published in Spanish as "Las oropéndolas" in *Una canción en la madrugada* by Editorial Costa Rica in San José, Costa Rica. © 1970 Quince Duncan. Translation © 1994 Zoe Anglesey.

"Monday" by Fernando Durán Ayanegui was originally published in Spanish as "Lunes" in *El último que se duerma y otros relatos*, 2d ed., by Editorial Alma Máter in San José, Costa Rica. © 1988 Fernando Durán Ayanegui. Translation © 1994 Kirk Anderson.

"In the Shadow of the Banana Tree" by Carlos Luis Fallas is excerpted from the novel originally published in Spanish as *Mamita Yunai* by Soley y Valverde, San José, Costa Rica © 1941; republished by Editorial Costa Rica in San José, Costa Rica. © 1986 Editorial Costa Rica. Translation © 1994 Will Kirkland.

"Bucho Vargas, Healer and Medicine Man" by Mario González Feo was originally published in Spanish as "Bucho, Curandero y Saludador" in *Anuario del cuento costarricense 1967* by Editorial Costa Rica in San José, Costa Rica. © 1968 Mario González Feo. Translation © 1994 Mark Schafer.

"A Leaf of Air" by Joaquín Gutiérrez was originally published in Spanish as *La hoja de aire* by Editorial Nascimento in Santiago, Chile, 1968; republished by Editorial Costa Rica in San José, Costa Rica. © 1968, 1985 Joaquín Gutiérrez. Translation © 1994 Carol Christensen.

"The Palmitero" by Max Jiménez was published in Spanish as "El Palmitero" in *Eljaúl* by Editorial Nascimento in Santiago, Chile. © 1937 Max Jiménez. Translation © 1994 Gabriel Berns.

"Pastor's Ten Little Old Men" by Carmen Lyra was originally published in Spanish as "Los diez viejitos de Pastor" in *Los otros cuentos de Carmen Lyra* by Editorial Costa Rica in San José, Costa Rica. © 1990 Carmen Lyra. Translation © 1994 Margaret Sayers Peden.

"Believe It or Not" by Carmen Naranjo was originally published in Spanish as "¿A que no me van a creer?" and is reproduced by permission of the author. © 1991 Carmen Naranjo. Translation © 1994 Barbara Paschke.

"When New Flowers Bloomed" by Carmen Naranjo was originally published in *When New Flowers Bloomed: Short Stories by Women Writers from Costa Rica and Panama,* edited by Enrique Jaramillo Levi and published by Latin American Literary Review Press in Pittsburgh, Pennsylvania. © 1991 Latin American Literary Review Press.

"The Lizard with the White Belly" by Yolanda Oreamuno was originally published in Spanish as "La lagartija de la panza blanca." All Rights Reserved. Reproduced by permission of Sergio Barahona Oreamuno. Translation © 1994 Pamela Carmell.

"The Spirit of My Land" by Yolanda Oreamuno was originally published in Spanish as "El espíritu de mi tierra." All Rights Reserved. Reproduced by permission of Sergio Barahona Oreamuno. Translation © 1994 Pamela Carmell.

Deeper Than Skin by Abel Pacheco was originally published in Spanish as *Más abajo de la piel* by Editorial Costa Rica in San José, Costa Rica. © 1972 Abel Pacheco. Translation © 1994 James Hoggard.

"The Blue Fish" by Julieta Pinto was originally published in Spanish as "El pez azul" in *Cuentos de la tierra* by Editorial Costa Rica in San José, Costa Rica. © 1963, 1976 Julieta Pinto. Translation © 1994 Angela McEwan.

"We Have Brought You the Sea" by Uriel Quesada was originally published in Spanish as "Te hemos traido el mar" in *Ese día de los temblores* by Editorial Costa Rica in San José, Costa Rica. © 1985 Uriel Quesada. Translation © 1994 Barbara Ras.

"The Adventure" by Samuel Rovinksi was originally published in Spanish as "La aventura" in *Anuario del cuento costarricense 1967* by Editorial Costa Rica in San José, Costa Rica. © 1968 Samuel Rovinksi. Translation © 1994 Will Kirkland.

"The Bongo" by Carlos Salazar Herrera was originally published in Spanish as "El Bongo" in *Cuentos de angustias y paisajes* by Editorial El Bongo in San José, Costa Rica. © 1947, 1988 María E. Salazar. Translation © 1994 James Hoggard.

"The Carbonero" by Carlos Salazar Herrera was originally published in Spanish as "El Carbonero" in *De amor, celos, y muerte: tres cuentos* by Editorial El Bongo in San José, Costa Rica. © 1989 Editorial El Bongo. Translation © 1994 James Hoggard.

"The Girl Who Came from the Moon" by José León Sánchez was originally published in Spanish as "La niña que vino de la luna" in *La cattleya negra* by Editorial Costa Rica in San José, Costa Rica. © 1967 José León Sánchez. Translation © 1994 Will Kirkland.

"Mystery Stone" by Rima de Vallbona was entitled "Misterio de piedra" in Spanish. This is its first publication and appears by permission of the author. © 1989 by Rima de Vallbona. Translation © 1994 Barbara Paschke.

"The Chumico Tree" by Rima de Vallbona was originally published in Spanish as "El árbol del chumico" in *Mujeres y agonías* by Arte Público Press-University of Houston in Houston. © 1986 Rima de Vallbona. Translation © 1994 Mary Gomez Parham.

CPSIA information can be obtained
at www.ICGtesting.com
Printed in the USA
LVOW03n1344110418
573020LV00003B/4/P